Leading the Crimson and Gray

THE

PRESIDENTS

OF

WASHINGTON

STATE

UNIVERSITY

Leading the
Crimson and Gray

THE
PRESIDENTS
OF
WASHINGTON
STATE
UNIVERSITY

WSU
PRESS

Washington State University Press
Pullman, Washington

Washington State University Press
PO Box 645910
Pullman, Washington 99164-5910
Phone: 800-354-7360
Email: wsupress@wsu.edu
Website: wsupress.wsu.edu

LIBRARY OF CONGRESS CATALOGING-IN-PUBLICATION DATA
Title: Leading the Crimson and Gray : the presidents of Washington State University.
Description: Pullman, Washington : Washington State University Press, [2019] | Includes bibliographical references and index.
Identifiers: LCCN 2018046032 | ISBN 9780874223651 (acid-free paper)
Subjects: LCSH: Washington State University—Presidents—Biography. | Washington State University—History.
Classification: LCC LD5731.W62 L43 2019 | DDC 378.797/39—dc23
LC record available at https://lccn.loc.gov/2018046032

Contents

Preface

THERE IS SOMETHING SPECIAL ABOUT BEING PART OF the Great Cougar Nation. Many people have asked "what is it about WSU that creates this Cougar Pride?" At the end of the last Comprehensive Campaign, "Because the World Needs Big Ideas," Julie Gardner, wife of the late John Gardner, then WSU Foundation CEO, and my wife were discussing this very topic. Julie suggested that it probably had something to do with leadership and the relationships the various leaders have had with the WSU community—faculty, staff, students, and alumni. Later that day when we were all together, Julie and my wife brought that idea to me and said "wouldn't it be neat to have a history of our leaders and their individual contributions to the creation of 'Cougar Pride'?" My first reaction was guarded, but the more Julie encouraged me to think about it the more the idea resonated with me. Many of us have been acquainted with our presidents both past and present. The question of how they have affected us and our institution's legacy, and how their leadership will, or already has, affected the future of the institution should be explored. This project's goal is to help us understand the answers to those questions and to imagine the future for WSU.

REGENT SCOTT CARSON

Foreword

IN LATE 2016, JUST A SHORT TIME AFTER MY ARRIVAL at WSU, Regent Scott Carson met with John Gardner, then CEO of the WSU Foundation, to discuss the possibility of developing a history of the leadership of our university focusing on the lives and work of our presidents. As Scott relates the story in his preface to this work, the inspired idea caught fire. John reached out to the staff at WSU Press, who in turn prepared a strategy for development of a book. Writers were recruited and research was begun. Soon manuscripts were submitted to the press for editing. Images were gathered and graphic artists engaged. The idea is now manifest in this book. We thank Scott for motivating us to undertake the creation of this work, and for providing the generous underwriting to support its publication.

When Washington State College opened its doors in January 1892, it was underfunded, undeveloped, and unappreciated by many, including legislators who saw the rural, land-grant institution as an unnecessary drain on state resources. Twenty-nine students entered the college's single building on the hill overlooking the town of Pullman that first day, most of them needing additional preparatory work before becoming eligible to enroll as freshmen. Our first president, George Lilley, served only nineteen months, unable to survive continuous battles with his Board of Regents. The term of his successor, John W. Heston, lowered the bar even further—he resigned after only nine months. Chaos reigned on college hill, and the infant institution's future was very much in doubt. But with the arrival of Enoch A. Bryan in summer 1893, the college finally found the leadership needed for a fledgling college. And those who followed Bryan as president have continued to sustain and inspire our institution.

These biographies, created by an outstanding gathering of WSU faculty, staff, graduate students, and alumni, reveal the unique challenges faced by leadership at a vibrant land-grant university for more than 125 years. Their interviews and deep research in the WSU archives, contemporary newspapers, and a variety of other sources illuminate the WSU family's everyday life and spotlight the intricacies of navigating institutional issues within often turbulent local, national, and international backdrops. University leadership's effective responses to these events expose the remarkable talents of those who have served WSU as president over the past dozen decades.

As we move forward, WSU will continue to face circumstances that challenge our goals and ideals. I have no doubt that we will succeed in meeting and mastering those challenges. I take pride in our university's efforts to achieve new levels of excellence as we pursue the Drive to 25, our goal to attain recognition as one of the nation's top 25 public research universities, preeminent in research and discovery, teaching, and engagement by the year 2030.

Leading the Crimson and Gray adds to our understanding and appreciation of WSU's history, growth, and contributions to our communities, state, and the world. The creative work and remarkable accomplishments of alumni, faculty, staff, and students at this university are an inspiration to all, and especially to me in helping shape the vision that will successfully carry forward the work of the presidents profiled in this book.

Go Cougs!
Kirk Schulz
Eleventh President of
Washington State University

Introduction

BY WILLIAM STIMSON

*W*HEN THE FOUNDERS OF THE UNITED STATES wrapped up their work and departed Philadelphia in 1787, they knew they had left an important matter unfinished. They had set up a marvelous, intricate system of government in which all important decisions devolved to citizens—but neglected to explain how citizens were supposed to know their part. George Washington, Thomas Jefferson, and James Madison, among others, worried for the rest of their lives that a plan to educate citizens in civic affairs was not tied into the new government system.

It didn't happen for a number of reasons. Initially it was priorities; there were so many things that needed to be done when the new government was launched. Then the founders discovered something about democracy they hadn't fully appreciated. In the old world of Europe, universities were funded by kings and dukes out of pocket change. In a democracy, citizens would have to tax themselves to support education. They did so willingly for elementary education, but a university, which few of them had ever seen, was something else. As an early study of the failure said, "It is difficult to convince the ordinary citizen that a university devoted to advanced study and research has any significance for him."[1] Finally, the question of a true federal university was caught up in the sectional jealousies that were already building toward a civil war.

Those who supported establishing a national university argued that it would help strengthen and unite the federal union, which was exactly what many Southerners did not want to happen.

The problem was finally resolved—a century later and in a way none of the founders could have anticipated. The biographies that follow help explain the solution. American higher education was fashioned, not in august halls of Philadelphia or Washington, DC, but in far-flung corners of the country, places like Lawrence, Kansas; College Station, Texas; Ames, Iowa; Fargo, North Dakota; and Pullman, Washington, where land-grant colleges were established. The colleges were financed by the federal government, but the federal government did not prescribe how they should be designed. With no detailed plan, those charged with opening the colleges had to figure it out for themselves. In the first chapter of this book we find that President George Lilley, with a budget of $2,000 and a mandate to get a college opened soon, helped shape the American higher education system. What kind of university should it be? Some, including the already established University of Washington on the western side of the state, advised it should become "the finest school of agriculture in the nation," but leave the rest of the state's higher education to the University of Washington. Enoch Bryan, the college's third president, decided the matter with the curriculum he put in place. All students would study American literature, history, foreign language, and chemistry. Bryan persuaded the state legislature to change the institution's name from Washington State Agricultural College and School of Science to Washington State College. It was a liberal arts college that taught agriculture among other things.

Similar decisions in similar land-grant institutions around the country gradually and inductively formed the American version of higher education. These new colleges drew on centuries of higher education tradition, naturally, but the American university had tasks the grand universities in Europe did not have—like dealing with democratic masses of students, and teaching them how to be participants in a democracy.

It is surprising how this makeshift, upside-down creation of a national higher education system somehow accomplished what Washington,

Jefferson, and Madison had hoped for. To appreciate this, one needs to recall the hopes of the founders.

IN THE SUMMER OF 1796, BENJAMIN LATROBE, A RECENT immigrant from Britain and later designer of portions of the capitol in Washington, DC, traveled to Mount Vernon to meet George Washington. Like many who met Washington for the first time, Latrobe left a record of the event. He found the man remarkable. "Washington has something uncommonly commanding and majestic in his walk, his address and his figure," Latrobe wrote in his diary. Yet, "There is a mildness about [his] expression and an air of reserve in his manner." Latrobe seemed surprised that, "He could laugh at a humorous observation and made several himself." Other times, "He is sometimes entirely silent for many minutes, during which time an awkwardness seemed to prevail in everyone present." They were waiting to hear what the general had to say.

Latrobe stayed the night at Mount Vernon to discuss architecture. After breakfast the next morning he was one of the circle of family members and visitors who surrounded the president as he talked. "His subject was principally the establishment of the university at the federal City [i.e., Washington, DC]." Washington said he had offered to donate several pieces of land he owned to the project. Other people had offered Congress money and plans for a university, but "there seemed to be no inclination to carry them into effect. He spoke as if he felt a little hurt upon the subject."

We know now what was bothering Washington. He was at this time corresponding with his closest advisor, Alexander Hamilton, about what to include in his annual address to Congress a few months hence. For five years he had been imploring Congress to fund a university "where the youth from all parts of the United States might receive the polish of erudition in the Arts, Science and Belle Letters." He wanted to state the case again in this last address, despite the slim chance of his words' success, to stress how important it was to him.

"What would render it of the highest importance, in my opinion," Washington wrote to Hamilton, "is that in the Juvenal period of life, when friendships are formed, and habits established that will stick by one, youth . . . would be assembled together and would by degrees discover that there was not that cause for those jealousies and prejudices which one part of the Union had imbibed against another part." Washington reminded his former artillery officer of how Revolutionary soldiers thought of themselves as Americans, not Southerners or Northerners. "What, but the mixing of people from different parts of the United States during the War rubbed off these impressions? A century in the ordinary intercourse would not have accomplished what the Seven years association in Arms did; but that ceasing, prejudices are beginning to revive again."

What Washington knew about educating youth he learned from commanding an army of young men. Their pay was bad and uncertain. The living conditions were horrible. There was no draft bringing replacements. To keep an army in the field, Washington had to lecture them regularly about larger goals, about honor, freedom, and democracy. After the miraculous victory at Trenton, soldiers were excited, exhausted, and anxious to go home because their enlistments were up. Washington's task was to persuade them to stay. He rode from regiment to regiment making his case. "My brave fellows, you have done everything I have asked you to do, and more than could be expected; but your country is at stake."[2] Washington—first in war, first in peace—was also first in teaching American civics.

Washington's idea of education meant personal, direct leadership. A famous example of this was the so-called Newburgh Conspiracy. Near the end of the Revolution, a contingent of his officers decided (justifiably) they were not being properly fed, equipped, and paid by the Continental Congress. They proposed to march on the Congress and make their demands. Washington could have ordered them to cease such talk or taken stronger measures. Instead he wrote a lecture. It was originally intended to be delivered as a letter to the insurgents, but he surprised them by showing up at their meeting to deliver it in person.

Washington claimed the right to speak as friend: "I have never left your side one moment [and] I have been the constant companion and witness of your Distresses." He swore he would seek the attention from Congress they were demanding. But, he said, the anonymous writer of the circular recommending rebellion was not calling for justice, but for "disserting our Country in the extremest hour of her distress. . . . My God! What can this writer have in view by recommending such measures. Can he be a friend to the Army? Can he be a friend of the country?"

At one point Washington drew out a letter of assurance from a member of the Continental Congress and read it aloud to the gathering. He had a hard time seeing the handwriting and pulled from his pocket a new pair of spectacles. "Gentlemen, you must pardon me. I have grown gray in your service and now find myself growing blind." This brought tears to the eyes of some officers. They knew it was true. By the time Washington finished and removed the glasses, the Newburgh Conspiracy was over.

THE COLLEGES THAT EVENTUALLY BECAME THE FEDERAL version of higher education were small and informal. Their presidents and professors had modest credentials themselves and in a small, isolated community, naturally fell into the role of mentors as well as professors. It was very much what Washington imagined higher education could be.

A dramatic example of the difference this made is the case of Glenn Terrell, president of WSU from 1967 to 1985. Though heading what was by then a sprawling, world-class institution, Terrell was known as "the students' president" because he made a point of being among them. In the spring of 1970 Terrill faced a rebellion something like Washington's Newburgh Conspiracy when hundreds of WSU students joined a national protest against the escalation of the Vietnam War. The campus in Pullman was one of many where students occupied buildings to demonstrate their frustrations and objections to federal actions. Many onlookers around the state suggested (or demanded) that Terrell expel these "spoiled children." Tall and courtly, a social psychologist and a veteran of World War II who had been at the Battle of the Bulge, Terrell engaged them in civic discourse. "The conversation that followed was remarkable," John Tappan Menard tells us in the biographic sketch in this book.

THOMAS JEFFERSON'S AIMS FOR HIGHER EDUCATION were very different from Washington's. Jefferson was less interested in a college that educated citizens than a college that trained a few to become scholars and scientists. Jefferson saw the university as an institution meant to instill knowledge for its own sake. He said, "a public Institution can alone supply those sciences which, though rarely called for, are yet necessary to complete the circle, all the parts of which contribute to the improvement of the country." By "sciences rarely called for" he meant the quest for knowledge for its own sake, pure science.

When Congress refused him as it had George Washington, Jefferson set out to do it himself. He spent the last years of his life planning and building the nation's first state university, the University of Virginia. He walked the site with rolled up plans under his arm, inspecting bricks, making pleas for support and donations, and lobbying legislators to distraction. Thomas Jefferson was the prototype of the state college president.

No matter how perfect the University of Virginia, though, it could never have achieved Jefferson's larger goal of giving the United States the scientific status of Europe. Europe's scientific community included a whole congregation of universities—Oxford, Cambridge, the Sorbonne, ten or twelve German universities, others scattered across Switzerland and Italy, plus many royal societies and institutes and technical colleges for specialized purposes. All of these were tied together in a single conversation through annual conferences, journals, letters, friendships, rivalries, and scientific clubs in nearly every city.

For example, the Lunar Society in Birmingham, England, included among its members James Watt, inventor of the steam engine—and therefore initiator of the age of mechanical power—and William Withering, a pioneer medical researcher who conducted controlled studies and identified the heart medicine digitalis.

Another member of the Lunar Society was Joseph Priestley, an eccentric cleric who had discovered how to create a purified form of air he named "oxygen." In 1774 he demonstrated his method of purification at a conference in Paris. One of those present, Frenchman Antoine Lavoisier, took Priestley's idea and placed it in a context of known basic elements, thus inventing the periodic table of elements. Lavoisier had a somewhat different idea about oxygen and he and Priestley engaged in a long argument that enlivened scientific discussions all across Europe. Lavoisier got the better of it, and his book, *A Treatise on the Fundamentals of Chemistry*, went into every library in Europe, a foundational work for potential chemists across the continent.

One such aspiring chemist, a bright teenager in England by the name of Humphrey Davy, read Lavoisier's book. One day a local man of science fell into conversation with Davy and was amazed by the teenager's grasp of chemistry. This mentor to Davy, Davies Giddy, who one day was to become president of the British Royal Society, remembered Davy and later recommended him for a position as administrator of the new Royal Institute, which would research applied science, including agriculture. Within a few years Davy would write *Elements of Agricultural Chemistry* (1813), replacing Lavoisier as the authority of chemistry.

In Germany, meanwhile, a marginally educated young man by the name of Justus Liebig attracted the notice of a local chemist and was invited to use the well-stocked library of a German noble, where he could read Priestley, Lavoisier, and Davy. Later a professor in Liebig's small university persuaded a local German noble, a patron of science, to send young Liebig to Paris to an all-European conference on chemistry. From that conference Liebig wrote back to a friend that his life changed as a result of what he saw in Paris. "It struck me like a bolt from the sky. The lectures of Gay-Lussac, Thenard, and the others are the cause of this." When Liebig returned to Germany he established a famous laboratory and wrote a book, *Chemistry in Its Applications to Agriculture*, which replaced Humphrey Davy's volume as the last word on organic chemistry.

All of this scientific activity was going forth in Europe while the U.S. Congress was hearing and turning down proposals for a national university year after year. As a consequence, the few young American chemists who could afford to go abroad took up studies in Liebig's lab or other such labs in Europe, but the vast majority drifted in other directions.

How could the United States ever duplicate the European scientific culture, the product of hundreds of years? In fact, it did. The Morrill Act of 1862 created, with the stroke of Abraham Lincoln's pen, more than 50 universities, each of them on the lookout for talented young scientists. A twin to the Morrill Act, the Hatch Act of 1887, added to each of those colleges a laboratory to investigate its agricultural problems. A few years later the Second Morrill Act tied all of the new state universities together with obligations to publish and circulate scientific findings. By the end of the nineteenth century, it was European students who were crossing the Atlantic to study in the United States.

JAMES MADISON'S INTEREST IN EDUCATION WAS AT FIRST less than that of colleagues Washington and Jefferson. That changed, however, as time went on and Madison began to worry that citizens were not prepared to carry out the duties of citizenship. The problem for Madison was that, as the nation grew, the numbers and types of voters were changing. His original idea was that voters would be only sober men with a stake in society, usually a farm or business. By the 1820s requirements for voting were being dropped in various states and it seemed that soon any citizen would be able to vote.

In 1822 a colleague in Tennessee wrote to Madison to describe what that state was doing about education and to ask Madison for advice.

Madison suggested that, along with reading, writing, and arithmetic, Tennessee invest in globes of the earth for every classroom. Just knowing of other countries "never fails, in uncorrupted minds, to weaken local prejudices, and enlarge the sphere of benevolent feelings." Madison wanted American children to look beyond their village. He complimented Tennessee on its attention to education and added: "A popular Government, without popular information, or the means of acquiring it, is but a Prologue to a farce or a tragedy; or perhaps both."

Madison soon witnessed the farce. The presidential election of 1828 became a spectacle of lies and smears. Republican papers spread rumors about Andrew Jackson's wife's virtue and his mother's race. The process was so shocking to Jackson's wife that he believed it caused her early death. On the other side, Democrats appealed to the new Irish immigrants by claiming that incumbent John Quincy Adams was anti-Catholic, which he was not.

Old-style Republicans did not know what to make of an "irrational zeal" they perceived in Jackson backers. When president-elect Jackson arrived at the White House to be sworn in, said Republican Senator Daniel Webster, he was greeted by "ten thousand upturned and exultant human faces, radiant with sudden joy." An election to pick a competent leader had somehow transmuted into a personality cult. "They really seem to think," Webster marveled, "that the country is rescued from some dreadful danger."[3]

Madison heard such stories and feared he was seeing the beginning of a reign of irrationality in the rational political system he had devised. But then, writes Madison biographer Drew R. McCoy, Madison had an inspiration. The effects of property ownership that once stabilized the political system could be replaced by education, "a potentially boundless reservoir of virtue." Education instead of property would be the thing that made citizens sagacious enough to lead the country. "The sage of Montpelier never succumbed to . . . despair. . . . With renewed emphasis on the power of education, especially, his republican faith endured."[4]

The most striking single difference between the American system and the European model was the percentage of young people who attended college. Only some of them were destined to become scientists, but all were destined to become citizens, and four years of studying world literature and history, writing essays and papers that were required to be based upon reason, and simply maturing in a diverse community, delivered what Madison hoped would rescue the political system he created. Madison's other wish also worked out. Eventually land as a stake in society became harder to attain, but by the early twentieth century hundreds of thousands of citizens were finding their stake in society in the form of a profession or the intellectual tools to thrive in the capitalist economy. The twentieth century spread the political plagues of communism and fascism to all corners of the world, but American society was hardly affected. Americans were convinced they could look forward to thriving in the system that already existed. This is exactly what Madison hoped for.

But that took time. Meanwhile, the tragedy Madison foresaw for democracy arrived in the form of a civil war. That calamity brought a willingness to re-think the purposes of the national government. President Abraham Lincoln said that the war's "leading object is to elevate the condition of men—to lift artificial weights from all shoulders to clear the path of laudable pursuit for all, to afford all an unfettered start, and a fair chance in the race of life."[5] The Civil War generation came to believe that government should not just protect rights, but also enable citizens to enjoy those rights. In the depths of the war, in July of 1862, President Lincoln signed three landmark bills that looked beyond the war: One to finish the national railroad that would bring people to the West, a "Homestead Act" to make Western farms affordable to citizens, and a third to create a Land Grant College Act to put federally-sponsored colleges in each state of the union.

Justin S. Morrill, the sponsor of the Land Grant Act, introduced his bill to the House of Representatives like this:

This bill proposes to establish at least one college in every State upon a sure and perpetual foundation, accessible to all but especially to the sons of toil, where all needful science for the practical avocations of life shall be taught, where the higher graces of classical studies nor that military drill our county now so greatly appreciates will be entirely ignored.

Morrill added: "The bill fixes the leading objects, but properly, as I think, leaves to the States considerable latitude in carrying out practical details."

That "considerable latitude" commissioned college presidents, like those profiled in this book, to fulfill the vision of the founders' educational component. An example is Ernest O. Holland, president of Washington State for the three decades that encompassed two world wars and a national depression. Through it all, Holland kept tuition virtually free because he was dedicated to giving as many young people a chance at a higher education as he could. He is a prime example of how presidents of state colleges went beyond administering and, in fact, molded the federal system. Abraham Lincoln could *say* young people should have an "unfettered start," but Ernest O. Holland could make it happen.

The same is true with all of the presidents described here. They saw education as Madison saw it, as a chance to improve not only the individual but the society. The two presidents who succeeded Holland faced the challenges of pulling the university into the complex post–World War II era, starting with the influx of thousands of returning GIs, for whom President Compton had to build, in a hurry, a virtual second campus. He promised no veteran of World War II would he turned away from WSU, and he kept the promise. "Compton's short six years at Washington State College witnessed a transformation unlike anything in the history of the institution," writes Larry Clark. Compton doubled classroom space, oversaw the building of a new library, and began construction of a new student union building. Then he was fired. His biography in this book provides a much deserved second hearing.

Compton's successor, C. Clement French, handled university regents more skillfully and completed the task of bringing Washington State

College into the modern world, resulting in the change of the school's name to Washington State University in 1959.

A special accomplishment of the American university, often forgotten, was to successfully meld intellectual life and common life. For all its accomplishments, the old university model in Europe was often an object of suspicion by outsiders. It was a place that produced unsettling new ideas and held itself apart from the community. The Frenchman founder of modern chemistry mentioned above, Antoine Lavoisier, died by guillotine in the hands of suspicious French mobs. His British collaborator, Joseph Priestly, was hounded out of England for his radical ideas. The worst case of this reactionary anti-intellectualism took place in the most intellectually advanced European nation, Germany. In the early twentieth century German mobs rejected learning and murdered millions of people to serve myths.

The United States did not suffer such sieges of anti-intellectualism. A good example of why is Sam Smith, WSU president from 1985 to 2000. He came from a background common to the mass of people, growing up poor and working in the fields of Salinas, California. The University of California, Berkeley, one of the original land-grant colleges, did what state colleges were supposed to do: discovered Smith's talents, awarded him a scholarship, and graduated a talented chemist. Smith learned the art of administration at another land grant college, Penn State, and then was appointed president of a land grant college in Washington. For 15 financially difficult years Smith was the face of the WSU, and his common touch is just one reason why the university enjoyed good relations with the community. The same was true of Bryan, Holland, French—in fact all of the presidents. They were not just university presidents, but popular local citizens.

Smith's successor, Lane Rawlins, set as one of his goals to make WSU the destination for the best students in the region. He raised money to endow complete "full-ride" scholarships for a Distinguished Regents Scholars Program. One recipient in the initial class was thinking of attending a California school (all of the recipients had many choices), but took a second look at WSU because of the scholarship. Beyond her scholarly training, she credited her WSU education with making her "an educated, critical thinking, engaged citizen." That would have thrilled James Madison.

Rawlins often referred to the university as "Washington state's University" because its mandate was to supply to the whole state whatever higher education it needed. For many years the State of Washington suffered from a shortage of doctors and limited space for training new ones to serve not only Washington, but a five-state area that had no medical schools. There were too few spaces at the Washington's existing medical school at the University of Washington and as a consequence many future doctors had to leave the region for their educations. Too often they did not return to practice. This was a state educational problem and thus the state college's responsibility.

But opening a new medical school was a daring step and difficult task. It was opposed by the University of Washington on the grounds that medical training was its traditional territory. The debate went on and on.

The last of the presidents described in this book, Elson Floyd, declared that the medical school had been discussed enough. "It's now time to act." Floyd launched a campaign to raise millions of dollars for the project. He continued to campaign for the school even following his diagnosis with what proved to be fatal cancer. Contenders on the other side of the state must wonder: Don't these people ever quit? The answer is no. Read their stories.

NOTES

1   Edgar Bruce Wesley, *Proposed: The University of the United States* (Univ. of Minnesota Press, 1936), 22.

2   Page Smith, *A New Age Now Begins: A People's History of the American Revolution*, 2 vols. (McGraw-Hill, 1976), 1: 829.

3   Page Smith, *The Nation Comes of Age: A People's History of the Ante-Bellum Years* (McGraw-Hill, 1981), 17.

4   Drew R. McCoy, *Last of the Fathers: James Madison and the Republican Legacy* (Cambridge University Press, 1989), 173.

5   James McPherson, *The War That Forged a Nation: Why the Civil War Still Matters* (Oxford University Press, 2015), 13.

George Lilley and John Heston
1891–1893

BY MARK O'ENGLISH

*W*HEN GEORGE LILLEY WAS HIRED AS THE FIRST president of the Washington State Agricultural College and School of Science, virtually nothing had been done toward creating the school. The state had authorized the formation of a land-grant college and set aside as the first year's funds just $2,000. On Monday, April 27, 1891, a locating commission announced Pullman as the site of the school, and four days later, on May 1, Lilley was announced as president.

Though unknown in Washington state at the time, Lilley seems a logical choice, given that from 1884 to 1886 he had served a similar role at the Dakota Agricultural College (today's South Dakota State University), taking that land-grant school from a standing start into an active and successful college. George Hopp of Sedro-Woolley was one of the five members of the WAC's newly appointed Board of Regents; he had worked with Lilley in a similar role in South Dakota. After leaving the Dakotas, Lilley had traveled to his wife's childhood home in Lowell, Massachusetts. Apparently Hopp sold him on the idea of the new college's presidency, and Lilley was not just present in Tacoma, but joined the regents' meeting only a few minutes after they officially hired him.

George Lilley, 1893.
Historic WSU Photographs Collection,
pc004b35lilley-1893cc. WSU Libraries
Manuscripts, Archives, and Special
Collections. WSU MASC.

Personal descriptions of George Lilley are few and far between. President E. A. Bryan describes him as "large, of very dark complexion, and quite deliberate in his speech and movements." Students described him as having a kindly nature, and he was well-liked by those in his classes. His few surviving letters show he was a skilled writer, but nonetheless Lilley apparently chose to avoid publicity, as much as possible, choosing to let the work of the university stand for itself.

Lilley was born in Kewanee, Illinois, on February 9, 1850, the second child of five born to moderately well-off English immigrants. His family owned several hundred acres of farm land, including a small coal mine. He was well educated, attending nearby Knox College from 1869 to 1873, the University of Michigan from 1873 to 1875, and Pennsylvania's Washington and Jefferson College from 1875 to 1878, where he received a master's degree. Apparently he received no degrees from his earlier schools. After 1878 he left academia for business, but continued working remotely, achieving a PhD in mathematics from Illinois Wesleyan in 1882 or 1883. In 1886 he received two honorary degrees, a master's degree from

Knox College, and an LLD (effectively a doctoral law degree) from Illinois' Chaddock College. The latter would eventually prove problematic when his detractors would confuse his earned PhD with his honorary LLD, incorrectly declaring the former honorary.

In 1878 Lilley entered business in Corning, Iowa, forming a partnership to purchase corn from local farmers and resell it to Chicago-based distributors. During this time he married Sophia Adelaide Munn; he and Adelaide had just one child, Frank, who died in infancy. While in Corning, Lilley befriended George Hopp, who published the local newspaper, a friendship which would prove significant throughout the rest of his life.

In June of 1884 Lilley was offered, and accepted, the presidency of the Dakota Agricultural College in Brookings, South Dakota. How and why Lilley received the position are lost to history, but it is worth noting that George Hopp, the newspaper publisher from Corning, was producing the Brookings paper, and was one of the community members serving on the board that arranged the construction of the first DAC buildings (effectively, a regent). That connection was almost certainly what brought Lilley to the school's attention, just as it would later bring Lilley to Washington state.

Though Lilley had been offered and had accepted the Dakota job, the first buildings had not yet been completed and he had little to do, and little likelihood of actually being paid. In order to complete the buildings and start the school, Lilley donated $500, one-third of his first year's salary, back to the school to complete the necessary structures.

President Lilley successfully started the school that September, and on a shoestring budget managed to recruit the first faculty, start a college program, and complete the first several buildings. However, in 1886 the state changed the Board of Regents system, and Lilley ran afoul of the new board. He was accused of being a lax disciplinarian, apparently a fair accusation as he set up a student committee to self-manage discipline, and it was incorrectly contended that his PhD was not an earned degree. He eventually resigned, but it seems the departure was fairly amicable as he remained as acting president until a new president was hired. He remained on staff afterward as professor of mathematics. However, in spring of 1890 a purge was conducted of much of the existing faculty, and in June Lilley was let go. Less than a year later, at the age of 41, he would become president of the Washington Agricultural College and School of Science.

When Lilley was appointed president of the WAC on May 1, 1891, the school was facing a pair of significant difficulties. For the initial year, the legislature had allocated a mere $2,000 to get the school up and running; the Board of Regents' expenses alone totaled over three-quarters of that. While Pullman had been awarded the college, numerous other cities and towns in eastern Washington had coveted it as well. Representatives of Yakima County, the second choice, threatened legal action, and soon sought an injunction against the regents. News of the injunction reached Pullman on May 22, literally as the regents were in a meeting to discuss plans for their first building. While "helpful" Pullman businessmen led the sheriff bearing the restraining order on a merry hunt around Pullman, the regents quickly signed and mailed off the necessary contracts for the initial building before the sheriff could find them. With that construction set in motion, the regents and Lilley accepted the restraining order and could do no further work.

Unable to act officially while the legal actions against the college were taking their course, Lilley left Pullman and set about quietly and unofficially contacting professional acquaintances about filling faculty positions. As a result, almost all of the WAC's initial faculty had South Dakota connections. Nancy Van Doren, preceptress and professor of English, had held similar positions dating to the opening of the Dakota Agricultural College. John O'Brien Scobey, agriculture, had been almost singlehandedly responsible for starting the DAC, to the point that not just a building but the entire county are now named after him. Charles Munn, veterinary science, was Lilley's brother-in-law and apparently had no teaching experience, but was a practicing veterinarian in Brookings. George Hitchcock, chemistry and physics, was a professor at the nearby

This very faded image is the only known photograph of the original six faculty members, taken in June 1892. President Lilley is center front, and clockwise from him are Scobey, Hitchcock, Van Doren, Munn, and Lake. The building at the left is the Crib; Pullman is behind them. *William Barkhuff Photographs, pc07f02n07. WSU MASC.*

Pierre University. The final member of the initial faculty, Edward R. Lake, horticulture, forestry, and botany, was a professor at the Oregon Agricultural College (today Oregon State University) before and after coming to Pullman; it is unclear what connection led him to the Pullman position.

When the various court cases finally came to a close in the college's favor, the regents decided to act quickly to forestall any further litigation. On November 16 they ordered Lilley to bring together a faculty and a plan of instruction, and for classes to begin in mid-January. With his small faculty in place Lilley decided to build on just two fronts: to focus on the "agricultural college" but to leave the "school of science" for the following year, and to get the experiment station, from which the college would derive its federal land-grant funds, up and running. While Professor Hitchcock was not able to leave his prior position and reach Pullman until spring term, the other faculty were in place on time, and on January 13, 1892, the Washington Agricultural College opened to the public, with a reported first term enrollment of about 60 students.

In focusing on the "agricultural college" portion of the college's charge, Lilley was recognizing one of the primary difficulties in western education. In contrast to the present day, high schools were almost non-existent in the 1890s, and Washington had only three in total at the time the WAC began. Those three were in the larger centers of population, far from Pullman. With most of his likely students possessing only a grade school education, much of the first year's instruction was set at a high school level, focusing either on preparatory classes which would bring the students up to a point at which they could enter college-level coursework, or on elementary courses intended to provide practical skills for students who would be returning to their farms rather than pursuing a college degree. The experiment station paralleled this, focusing on research to benefit farmers and ranchers in the northwest, as well as outreach intended to provide instruction on how to improve their agricultural practices.

Again, however, financial difficulties beset the college. Though the legislature's allotted funding for the combined 1892 and 1893 years was well over the $2,000 of the previous year, the college was $2,600 in debt at the start of 1892 and had been putting off payments to try to stay ahead. Money was due to the college from the federal government, but the bureaucratic hoops to be jumped through and the time delay in communicating with Washington, DC, meant the money was months behind; the first payment from federal funds would not arrive until March of 1892. Nonetheless, the college started a second instructional building, a dormitory, created a reservoir and other support facilities

This November 1893 photo of campus is the only "true" image from those early years. There is another, closer, full campus photo, supposedly from 1893 and much used over the years; however, it is actually fake—someone took an 1895 photo, cropped it carefully, and then scratched three newer buildings off to create an "1893" view of campus. Left to right are the Crib, the original College Hall, the first Ferry Hall, and the shops/power plant and the mechanical building. *Historic WSU Photographs Collection, pco04b14f1893-99_1893-11. WSU MASC.*

during this timeframe, and set plans in place for two branch experiment stations elsewhere in the state. Attendance at the college grew dramatically, from an initial first-day attendance of 29 (and quickly to the full 59 or so of the initial enrollment), up to 130 by the end of spring term, and then to approximately 300 by fall of 1892.

Sometime in spring of 1892 dissatisfaction began to spring up within the Board of Regents, which came close to killing the newborn college. The five regents had been appointed in spring 1891 by lieutenant governor Charles Laughton (governor Elisha Ferry being ill), and most if not all were political appointees, members of a Republican party that strongly controlled the state but was subject to serious infighting. Of the initial five appointees, one, Jacob Bellinger of Colfax, had joined the committee before the location of the school was set, but then stopped attending meetings once Pullman was selected. The other four were Lilley's old friend George

Hopp, Simon B. Conover of Port Townsend, Eugene Fellows of Spokane, and Andrew Smith of Tacoma. While initially all seemed well with the four who attended meetings, Smith soon seemed to sour on the process. Matters came to a head in summer when Smith objected to, but was out-voted on, plans for the initial College Hall (subsequently torn down in 1907 and not to be confused with the current College Hall). Construction of the building expended more funds than the school had available. Smith also objected to expenditures on chemistry supplies because a firm from his side of the state had not been allowed an opportunity to bid.

Effectively, a coup took place within the board that summer. Each regent was required to have a $50,000 bond in place, and Governor Ferry, or someone close to him, apparently arranged to have the person who had supplied Hopp's bond withdraw it. Hopp promptly found a new source for the money, but in the interim the governor replaced him with a new regent, one approved by Smith: Daniel Lesh of Yakima (the town which had sued the state in hopes of preventing the college from being placed in Pullman). At the same time, the absentee Jacob Bellinger was convinced to come to meetings, and the coalition of Smith, Lesh, and Bellinger effectively seized control of the five-man board. Bellinger then wrote the governor inquiring about the legal necessities for removing the college from Pullman, but apparently nothing came of his inquiry.

Almost immediately Smith began publicly campaigning against Lilley through the press, appealing to the public with statements such as questioning why Lilley's faculty were all from out of state—weren't Washingtonians good enough to teach at their own college? However, Simon Conover, the board's elected president, cautioned his fellow regents against taking any action to replace President Lilley for fear of disrupting the school's development. At the next meeting, the threesome of Smith, Lesh, and Bellinger set in place bylaws incorporating a rule stating that the president of the board could only vote in a tie, effectively neutralizing Conover's vote.

Back in February, during a Board of Regents meeting in Tacoma, Conover had apparently been pulled aside by a man from Iowa claiming

The Crib, the first campus
building, ca. 1891–1892.
*Historic WSU Lantern
Slides, pc006b01n041.
WSU MASC.*

to have information about Lilley's prior business transactions and about
his character. In March Conover exchanged letters with John Bixby, the
county attorney based in Lilley's former residence of Corning, Iowa.
Lilley had held a contract there with a Chicago-based firm, Dows, to
purchase corn from Iowa farmers and sell it to that firm. Once he
started purchasing corn, the firm wrote him not to ship, as they were
not yet ready to accept it. Knowing there was going to be much more
corn available to fill his contract with Dows, Lilley sold the corn he was
holding to someone else. Dows claimed this was theft of their property
and the case did eventually go to trial, with Lilley found not guilty. In
association with these events, several other charges were made, none of
which went to trial. Bixby, who had been prosecuting attorney, made
additional general accusations against Lilley in his letters to Conover,
including that Lilley had gone into hiding for long periods to avoid
prosecution, that he had defrauded the people he purchased corn from,
and that he had "made witnesses disappear." With apparently nothing
to go on but unsupported accusations and the fact that Lilley was found
not guilty, Conover had passed the information on to the governor but
otherwise let it lie. At their September meeting, however, Governor
Ferry directed the regents to address the accusations, and the vague
slanders against Lilley were made public. President Lilley asked for,
and was given, a few weeks leave to go back to Corning and bring back

proof of his innocence, but subsequently was never allowed to present his information at any future board meeting.

At the November board meeting, in Pullman, the salary of the college president was reduced by over 30 percent, but no further action was taken on Lilley. Some contend that the regents thought that making a decision to remove Lilley while meeting in Pullman would have held negative consequences for them; the next meeting was set for December in Yakima.

By this point, the writing was clearly on the wall. The students in Pullman came together and sent a petition to the Board of Regents, nearly unanimously signed, asking that Lilley be retained. A December 12 meeting, attended only by Bellinger, Lesh, and Smith (Lilley himself was stuck in Pullman, bedridden with pneumonia), was spent handling routine business and reading and discussing applications for the presidency. It should be noted that before Lilley was hired, it was written that the president's "term of office shall be for one year and until his successor shall be elected and qualified." No grounds were required to remove him; the board could simply elect a new president after one year of service. On December 13, 1892, with Conover also present, they did so. A vote was held and they appointed John Heston, principal of Seattle High School, as the new president. The vote was not unanimous. Conover voted to retain Lilley and the other three split votes between Heston and J. P. Hendricks, also of Seattle. At this point the regents also made the decision to fire Professor John Scobey. No reason was given; presumably his history and friendship with Lilley was reason enough. Professor George Hitchcock, alarmed and with an offer in hand from a California college, also resigned within the week.

These actions could have been handled quietly and with a modicum of decorum, protecting the school. However, Regent Smith chose to publish, in multiple newspapers around the state, a slate of accusations against Lilley, very publicly making a case that the college was mismanaged and in poor shape. Lilley would in turn make an equally public reply to the newspapers over a week later, after he'd recovered. Among the arguments, Smith contended that Lilley's financial books were poorly kept and nothing could be determined from them; Lilley countered that the college's newly hired accountant had found them satisfactory and continued Lilley's system rather than changing it, and that any need of Smith's for information from the books had been answered promptly. Smith contended Lilley had morally failed to prevent questionable excess expenditures on campus buildings and supplies; Lilley pointed out that it was the Board of Regents that made those contracts, not him. Smith contended that there were no letters as evidence from Lilley's hiring of the initial faculty; Lilley responded by sharing those letters. Smith argued that the faculty should only have been paid from the start of school, not their terms of hire; Lilley provided the board's decisions showing otherwise (admittedly, according to both parties, the decisions were confusing, but Smith had not contested them at the time). Smith contended Lilley had made a dishonorable request for parts of his salary that were being delayed (though already approved and ultimately granted); Lilley suggested that this was just a way to work around the objections of a "hyper-critical state office to the payment of an honest debt." Smith said that Conover had told him he was "so tangled up" with Lilley that he was constrained against voting against him, an accusation that both Conover and Lilley denied. Finally, Smith decried the overcrowded condition of the school dormitory; Lilley pointed out that it was constructed to the board's specifications (with Smith as head of the responsible subcommittee), and that when Lilley had informed them of the problems in admitting all the applying students, the regents had replied for him to "accept all applicants; we will provide sufficient accommodations."

On Tuesday, December 20, Lilley met with students for the first time since his illness and release, addressing a meeting of the Websterian Society, a campus debating organization. He commended the students for their petition, spoke against the reply of the regents ("we as the Board of Regents of the said college will exercise our very best judgment in the matter and do what we think will be for the best interest of the students as well as the college") as dismissive, and encouraged the students to stand for their own rights and for them to express those rights in the proper manner.

The following morning was the final day of the term. Lilley and the faculty were present at the school's morning chapel, as was Regent Smith, who had brought President Heston for his introductory visit to the campus. Prior to the arrival of the faculty, the students were heard to be altering lyrics to their morning music practice, reportedly replacing the words to the song *John Brown's Body* with lines such as "We'll hang Regent Smith on a sour apple tree" and "we'll have George Lilley as our next president." When chapel started, Lilley and the other two departing faculty members, with Smith and Heston watching, proceeded to give short farewell addresses. Lilley spoke last and answered Smith's recent accusations that he had misappropriated student funds, interrupting himself to hush the students when they called out Smith during the talk. Smith and Heston departed to a side room rather than face the students, and so Lilley closed with "Merry Christmas" and best wishes for the school and the new president. While Lilley was inside afterwards sharing personal goodbyes, Smith and Heston stepped outside, where departing angry students pelted them with debris. Stories told in later years about the event mention eggs, rotten eggs, cabbages, snowballs, and dirt clods as being among the items to hit the pair, but in fairness to the students few if any eggs, certainly none rotten, appear to have been present. The mention of cabbages likely comes from the fact that a cabbage field was located outside the building, but it seems unlikely that much cabbage remained on the ground by mid-December. Snowballs and dirt clods are a certainty, however. The mention of eggs appears to come from students reportedly gathering outside the train station later that day in an attempt to egg Regent Smith, but he did not show and no egging occurred there. Further, though reports faulted the students for attacking their incoming president, they later defiantly denied having done so, stating that they had nothing against President Heston, having never met him and knowing little of him. Smith, on the other hand, they confessed to going after, but he unfortunately attempted to hide behind the taller Heston. In any case, the pair had fled down the hill into town, taking refuge behind locked doors in their hotel rooms.

Cabbage field, with Ferry Hall under construction
in the background, summer 1892.
Historic WSU Lantern Slides, pc006b01n002. WSU MASC.

The students' attack on Smith and Heston made headlines around the state, bringing the turmoil at the state college solidly into the public eye and creating a black mark which would last for years. While much fault was placed upon the students, blame began to be laid against the actions of the Board of Regents, at least partially due to the public statements of both Smith and Lilley. With the current governor, Elisha Ferry, about to leave office, and a new one about to come in, pressure would be placed upon that new governor, John McGraw, to do something about the conditions at the state college.

IN A BETTER WORLD, JOHN HESTON'S SAD INTRODUCTION to the Washington Agricultural College and School of Science would be the low point of his presidency. Unfortunately, it didn't get significantly better. The regents were about to be investigated (and ultimately

John William Heston, date unknown.
*Historic WSU Photographs Collection,
pc004b35heston, WSU MASC.*

removed), his school was in debt, his students resented him, and the
public now held a very negative public opinion of him. A national economic panic that began in February of 1893 certainly did not help.
Heston never really had a chance.

John William Heston had been born at Pine Grove Mills, Pennsylvania, on February 1, 1854. His father was a cabinet maker and Heston had
little time for school as a child, being needed for farm work. At the age
of 20 he entered the preparatory program at nearby Pennsylvania State
College, completing that program before entering college-level classes.
Heston received a bachelor's degree in 1879 and a master's degree in 1882,
both from Penn State. In 1881 he married Mary Ellen Calder, daughter
of the former president of the college; the couple would have two sons.
Heston was principal of the college's Preparatory Department from 1879
to 1887, and then a professor of pedagogics from 1887 to 1890. In 1890 he
left Penn State and moved west to Washington state, reportedly for his
health, and became principal of Seattle High School, where he remained
until hired away by the state college.

Because Heston was very much a self-made man, it is clear the regents could see him as a fit for the college as it stood. Though young—just 39 and described as looking ten years younger—Heston was a noted disciplinarian where Lilley had been seen as lacking control over his charges. With only a minimal college program in place so far, Heston's experience in preparatory education and high schools fit the immediate needs, though he was not necessarily best suited for its future. Heston's stated goals, however, were quite aspirational, calling for the elimination of the preparatory school and for training students not just in agriculture but in mechanical, electrical, and mining engineering—all fields with real world applications. He specifically wanted the college to be a "practical school," not a "literary school."

With Smith's trio still in solid control of the Board of Regents, virtually all decisions ran through them, and through the Seattle political bosses with whom Smith associated. Heston had little say in hires and other decisions; when his rival for the presidency, J. P. Hendricks, was appointed professor of agriculture, all Heston could do was keep working as best he could. This imbalance in power would last until early in Heston's successor's term; E. A. Bryan described the early president's role as that of a "secretary and amanuensis" to the regents. One indication of their respective statuses could be seen in the practice, as seen in the minutes of the board, of referring to the elected head of the Board of Regents as "president," and to the college president as "professor."

On January 19, 1893, with new politicians in place after the 1892 elections, a joint committee composed of three state senators and four representatives was authorized to thoroughly review "all matters pertaining to the Agricultural College and School of Science." Among the accusations leveled against the college and its administrators, past and present, were old stories of bribery in the placement of the college, the hiring of faculty for political rather than educational reasons, excessive expenditures for supplies, inappropriate spending on buildings, and much more. Some were clearly true, notably the case of E. L. Newell, who had applied as a music professor and who Regent Smith's Seattle-based political bosses had pushed him to hire. With no music position available they instead made him professor of civil engineering, despite his having no knowledge whatsoever of the field; the Spokane newspapers would begin referring to him as "the musical prodigy." Most of the accusations, however, were less obviously true and required more investigation. The commission set about a long study of the Pullman school.

With the status of the college up in the air pending the committee's reports, the regents stopped meeting as of January 18. Anything up to and including the moving or closing outright of the college was a possibility. The immediate effect on the campus and classwork was minor, save that college faculty went unpaid as there was no Board of Regents to authorize those outlays; morale suffered. Heston began spending most of his time in Olympia, lobbying or meeting politicians, and rather than move to Pullman, his wife and sons remained in their Seattle home while Heston simply took a room in the men's dormitory on campus.

In the first week of March 1892, the committee finally returned their report. It examined sixteen points of concern and came back with four recommendations. The important points were: they found the location in Pullman to be fully satisfactory; a large allocation of funds (over $160,000, a far cry from that initial 1891 allocation of $2,000) should be made to cover the existing debts and to provide sufficient buildings to get the campus firmly and permanently established; and, though no criminal fault was found in their behavior, the current Board of Regents was to be considered not confirmed by the legislature, and so dismissed.

While the results of the committee's work were, in the long-term, excellent for the college and the city of Pullman, none of it proved immediately helpful to Heston. By the end of March the governor had appointed new regents, but Heston only learned of their appointments and their names from the local newspaper as the governor did not see fit even to notify him. Learning from the prior mistakes, this board was created to be less political, and was split close to evenly among the political parties of the day. Four of the five committee members were from eastern Washington, slightly separating the Board of Regents from Seattle politics and politicians. Once appointed, the new regents required confirmation before they could act, and so not until May 4, in Pullman, did the new board meet and begin the job of "sweeping clean" the problems created by the former regents. Though no initial animus between Heston and the Board of Regents seems present through reading of the minutes or the local newspapers, nonetheless on May 6 Heston submitted his resignation, which was accepted effective June 30 (later moved back to August 31 to allow the regents more time to locate and bring in his successor). Heston remained in his position during this time, seeing to the day-to-day running of the school and attending the board's meetings, but it is hard to say what role, if any, he actually played in their larger decisions. Nonetheless, he remained the public face of the school, even facing anger from the students after the regents fired Professor J. P. Hendricks, Heston's former rival for the presidency. Despite the influx of state funding, the Board of Regents and President Heston still faced financial difficulties when former Regent Smith, who had been acting as treasurer for the first board, refused to acknowledge either his own removal or the authority of the new board. Unfortunately, the college's federal checks continued to be mailed directly to Smith, who refused to turn that money over to the college. Smith would take the state to court over his removal, and it would take until August 2, 1894, almost a year after Heston's departure, for the college to finally receive the money that Smith withheld.

On July 22, 1893, the Board of Regents concluded its search for a new president, selecting Enoch Albert Bryan of Vincennes, Indiana, out of a pool of 13 candidates. With Heston eyeing the door and a more sympathetic board in place, former president Lilley, still living in Pullman, actually applied to the regents for a faculty position. The regents contacted Bryan for his opinion on the matter and he, not knowing Lilley but still expressing sympathy for his circumstances, suggested it might be better for the college if old issues were not resurrected. Lilley's application was politely rejected.

On August 28 John Heston departed Pullman to return to his Seattle home after just eight and a half months as president, finally free of the mess he'd inherited. That afternoon his successor, E. A. Bryan, arrived in Pullman and assumed the reins of the college.

LILLEY AND HESTON HAD ONE FINAL UNFORTUNATE moment in the Pullman spotlight in early 1894, when former agriculture professor John Scobey made a report, the source of which was kept anonymous, to Governor McGraw claiming various instances of poor money handling by the current Board of Regents. The governor, on an eastern Washington trip, visited Pullman to talk with President Bryan about the complaints and, missing Bryan by a few hours, asked Bryan's secretary to give him access to the board's minutes. When Bryan learned that the secretary had done so, Bryan fired him. The governor appointed a neutral investigator, but when the two men who had initially agreed to sign the complaints (local businessmen S. A. Mudge and A. J. Fariss) declined to do so without first consulting with a lawyer, the investigator ended up leaving Pullman without conducting any useful research. Mudge and Fariss, it should be noted, had been associated with people responsible for building the original College Hall and campus reservoir. Both had suffered cost overruns for which they felt they had never been fully reimbursed; both the prior and the current board had rejected those requests for payments. Former president Heston would eventually sign on to the anonymous complaints; the investigation would ultimately note small flaws but clear the regents of wrongdoing.

The *Pullman Herald* spent several months placing the blame for the anonymous complaints on former president Lilley. President Bryan, in his annual report to the governor, described 1894 as "marked by the triumphant victory of the College over the forces of evil that beset it" (though Bryan was certainly referencing Smith's hijacking of the treasury as among those "forces"). In Bryan's own history of the college, he describes daily attacks on the college administration by the *Olympia Tribune* (owned by Scobey), but few if any such attacks actually appear in that paper during this time. While it's certainly impossible to determine any "blame" for the accusations nearly 125 years later, it should be noted that Scobey and Lilley were investors in the *Pullman Tribune*, a rival newspaper, and that Fariss and Scobey ran for political positions in opposition to the factions with which the *Herald*'s editor was allied. For the duration of the election season, the *Herald* screamed headlines like "Tyranny; Pullman and her Institutions Endangered by a Band of Conspirators; They Seek to Tear Down and Destroy the Best Interests of the City," and proceeded to drag up all the old accusations against Lilley. After repeated comparisons to Satan, Lilley apparently sought legal protection from the paper, an action the *Herald* promptly denounced on the front page as "Press Censorship!" The *Herald* ceased, or at least drastically reduced, the volume of its attacks after the spring, and in summer Lilley departed Pullman to accept a role as principal at Park School in Portland, Oregon.

After a few years at the Park School, Lilley became professor of mathematics at the University of Oregon, where he would remain until his death from arteriosclerosis in 1904. His math textbooks, the first of which he completed in 1891 while waiting for permission to open Pullman's college, were well-received and remained in use for years. His wife Adelaide is still remembered in Eugene as one of the founders of their public library and as their first librarian.

John Heston returned to Seattle after leaving the state college, and passed through a succession of positions including principal of a local school, lawyer, president of the short-lived University of Seattle (which, before closing in 1894, honored him with an honorary PhD in law despite never graduating any actual students beyond a high school level), and superintendent of the Everett Board of Education. In 1896 he left the state for good, becoming the third president of the Dakota Agricultural College, the same school George Lilley had started twelve years earlier. In 1903 Heston moved 40 miles southwest to accept the presidency of the Madison State Normal School (today's Dakota State University), where he would remain until his 1920 death from a stroke. At those two schools Heston found the opportunities he never had in Pullman, and today both schools credit his leadership with expanding them and carrying them into a modern era of instruction. Dakota State University's administration building, Heston Hall, is named in his honor.

It is perhaps unfair to both men to view Lilley and Heston together, given that all they really had in common were a short time in Pullman helping launch a college, and their antagonistic boards. Certainly Lilley deserves credit not just for starting the college from nothing and building it into a going concern, but for building a camaraderie and community within the student body to the point that the several hundred students would almost unanimously come to his support against those wanting him out. At the same time, however, Lilley's reticence to speak for himself or for the school made it easy for those who opposed him or the school to place words in his mouth. As an educator, Lilley inspired those around him and motivated his students and faculty to success, but in political matters he failed to find ways to work with those who ended up opposing him. One has to suspect that Lilley learned from his experiences in Pullman, happily finishing his career in Oregon as a "mere math professor."

Heston, on the other hand, certainly doesn't deserve the blame for the frailties of the college in his brief time. Attendance, peaking at close to 300 under President Lilley, fell dramatically after Smith's public attacks, the removal of the popular Lilley, the student assault on Smith and Heston, and the negative press preceding the dismissal of the former board, with which Heston's name was firmly associated in the public mind. By the time incoming President Bryan started the 1894 fall term, attendance was a mere 30 students. However, it's hard to imagine what Heston could have done differently, and he kept the university running despite its employees going unpaid for close to four months and massive student dissatisfaction. Under a new board and with new funding he was present as planning began for the new Administration Building (today known as Thompson Hall) and several other structures. Based on his later correspondence with President Bryan, Heston clearly had difficulties with some members of the new Board of Regents, but he kept these out of the press until almost a year after leaving office. As seen through his successes as president of two South Dakota colleges after leaving the state, Heston was a visionary leader and a more than qualified administrator and politician, but unfortunately the circumstances in Pullman prevented him from ever putting those skills to work in doing more than keeping the college alive.

RESEARCH NOTES

One of the difficulties in researching this period in time is the lack of surviving original materials originating with either Lilley or Heston. Lilley's papers were destroyed in a fire within six years of his death; Heston left little. Neither published much, Lilley's math textbooks excepted. We are forced instead to look at the effects of their actions, and at the writings of those near them. The following suggested resources cover this time period.

A meeting by meeting account of college decisions, hirings, firings, contracts, etc. can be found in the WSU Board of Regents' Minutes, 1891–1894 (WSU MASC, Archives 257, Volume 1).

Original documents from Lilley's Iowa legal difficulties can be found in the S. B. Conover papers (WSU MASC, Cage 692, Box 1, Folder 11), and additional materials in that collection deal with Conover's tenure as a regent.

The Ferry/McGraw Papers (WSU MASC, Cage 435) comprise photocopies of official state documents from those two governors, relating to early college business.

President E. A. Bryan's Papers (WSU MASC, Archives 158). While the outgoing correspondence in Box 1 is of little interest, the alphabetical incoming correspondence in boxes 28–54 contains materials from presidents, regents, faculty, and others from this time period. Limited materials from Lilley's and Heston's tenures are also included.

A newspaper scrapbook in the William Barkhuff Collection (WSU MASC, PC 7, folder 13) provides a student-centric view of the 1892 firing of Lilley, and is one of the few places both Smith's arguments against

Lilley and Lilley's reply can be found. Newspaper scrapbooks in the WSU Publications Scrapbook series (WSU 177) consist of clippings collected by the university, and tend to be one-sided.

WSU Publications: President's Office (WSU MASC, WSU 132) and Regents' Office (WSU MASC, WSU 140) each include the results of an attempt by the college in the 1940s to collect as much biographical information on individual regents and presidents as could be found at that time.

The College Record (January 1892 to April 1893) and *Evergreen* (March 1895 to present) were campus student newspapers and provide an invaluable record of campus events, and are available digitally through WSU MASC. The *Pullman Herald* is searchable online through the Library of Congress' Chronicling America, though the year 1892 is lost to history. The *Pullman Tribune* in this era, unfortunately, no longer exists. The *Spokane Spokesman-Review* and *Spokane Chronicle* are also often of use for these years. Microfilm of the *Tacoma Daily Ledger* (held at the Washington State Library) appears to be the best resource for Regent Smith's side of the Lilley/Smith conflict.

E. A. Bryan's own *Historical Sketch of the State College of Washington, 1890–1925* is the defining book on this period, and George Frykman's *Creating the People's University: Washington State University, 1890–1990* also provides insight. For a look at Washington state politics outside the college, see Robert Ficken's *Washington State: The Inaugural Decade, 1889–1899*.

Enoch A. Bryan
1893–1915

BY TIM STEURY

*"I clearly perceive that it is
utterly impossible for
the State College to be
separated from me,
or me from it."*

THE MORNING OF AUGUST 28, 1893, FOUND ENOCH A.
Bryan aboard a train from Spokane to Pullman, on his way to a
fledgling agricultural college he later acknowledged he'd never heard of
before being nominated as its president. He was mesmerized by the landscape and activity scrolling by his window. "The Palouse country was a
revelation and an inspiration," he writes in his *Historical Sketch of the State
College of Washington*. "I had known prairies but none where the endless
wheat fields of ripened grain rolled away like the waves of the ocean."

He marveled at the "odd looking headers" (harvesters) being pushed
instead of pulled across the hillsides by teams of horses, at the grain
wagons waiting in long lines at grain warehouses. "Rosalia, Oakesdale,
Garfield, Palouse all appeared to be full of life and motion and the train
was loaded with people coming and going."

Enoch A. Bryan, ca. 1892.
Historic WSU Photographs Collection,
pc004b35fbryan_86-0005. WSU MASC.

That afternoon, having been met at the station by members of the Board of Regents, Bryan relaxed briefly on the porch of the Palace Hotel, located where the Audian Theater now stands on Main Street, and reflected on what he'd seen so far of this place in which he had landed.

Downtown Pullman bustled. The county teacher's institute was in session in the auditorium of the new high school. Down the street a platform with rows of rough plank benches was the stage for the county temperance convention, while a selection of saloons around town offered a lively reason for the convention. All the wheat wagons seemed to have followed him to town and now stretched in long lines at the grain warehouses.

Bryan noted the Artesian Hotel, just as busy as the Palace, the First National Bank, the Pullman State Bank, Williams and Moss's planing mill, the Northern Pacific stockyards, and a flour mill. Only later did Bryan learn that many of the town's apparently thriving businesses were either in receivership or on the verge of bankruptcy. Only momentarily did Bryan believe that just maybe he had left the Panic of 1893 back east.

Indeed, in spite of first appearances, late summer 1893 was not an auspicious time in which to accept the challenge of building a state college out of the chaos of its first two years. One must wonder what it was that convinced Bryan to leave a respectable and comfortable position as president of the two-year Vincennes University in southern Indiana for eastern Washington, a state barely older than the fledgling Washington State Agricultural College, Experiment Station, and School of Science.

He must have sensed a wide-open promise in that rambling title. Bryan was 38 years old. Surely he suspected that he would never again be handed such an opportunity—and challenge.

Now, with a few minutes to himself on the porch of the Palace Hotel, in spite of the determination and self-assurance that would define his leadership, he must have been unable to keep a few doubts from entering his mind.

"As from the long shady porch of the hotel," he wrote in his *Historical Sketch*, "I looked up to the dry barren hilltop in the distance the gaunt outlines of old Ferry (not then so named) and the square red College hall—no trees or shrubbery about—the campus looked like an unreal scene, a thing strangely in contrast with the ideal seat of learning.

"And strikingly in contrast," he continued, "with the turreted castle which I had seen pictured in the advertising pamphlet at the Columbia Exposition in Chicago." That pamphlet pictured an enormously extravagant architectural artifice dreamed up by the first Board of Regents, a castle that was never more than aspirational and was firmly nixed by the state legislature.

"At any rate I was now face to face with the problems which had lured me into the West to accept the presidency—namely the building of a great state college in one of the last states in which such an institution was to be established."

But his college's potential was presently at best distant. "These evidences of a temple of learning about to be reared," he wrote, "looked very distant, very isolated, very lonesome."

Bryan's interlude on the porch of the Palace, his respite and opportunity for reflection, was soon cut short, perhaps strategically, for had he been allowed too much time for reflection, he may well have boarded the next train back to Indiana. But now he must go and meet the townspeople.

"There I was greeted by a multitude of citizens interested in seeing the individual who had the temerity to tackle the problem at which two presidents had failed."

On the stage of the high school auditorium, which was filled to capacity, Bryan was introduced by the president of the regents.

"I have always imagined that my first appearance in Pullman was not very impressive," wrote Bryan, "although the audience did, as a matter of fact, receive me very kindly."

"I was a small man," he continued, unsure of his impression on the crowd, "weighing about 130 pounds, wearing a full beard to add age and dignity and must have been somewhat disappointing in appearance on this my inauguration."

Bryan noted that he later overheard a man comment that he "allowed me about six months to run my course."

"My address was of necessity extempore in which role I have never rendered very satisfactory service. . . . Then descended from the high platform to the common level to shake hands with the citizens who greeted me kindly and sincerely and with whom I have lived happily ever afterward."

"THE PEOPLE I MET WERE CORDIAL AND APPARENTLY cheerful," Bryan recalls of his first meeting with the full Board of Regents. But he would soon find that they were barely hiding their anxiety and despondency over the straits of the young school. Without burdening their new president excessively, they started to lay out what he now faced.

First, the dining hall was deep in debt.

The Board informed me that it was in litigation concerning $19,000 of the Morrill fund for that year and did not know when it would become available; that it had already spent the year's installment of the state fund for fuel and incidental expenses, and that no further money would be available from that fund until the first of the following April. . . .

I learned that the College had opened its doors on January 13, 1892, in a little building on the top of the hill dubbed 'the crib' which was no longer used for college classes. I learned that in the remainder of the spring of 1892 and the following fall there had been a goodly influx of students, of proper age but backward in preparation. I learned that the five-story brick dormitory had been built and the three-story wooden structure for classes, etc., and that both had been finished late in the fall of 1892; that the finances were in a woefully bad condition; that in the summer of 1892 the Board and the first president had become antagonistic; that in the fall of 1892 they had elected a new president; that the 2nd president had served actively from January till May 1893; that the Board had been removed by the Legislature; that a new board (the one that had just elected me) had been appointed; that it found things in a bad mess, including the faculty; that it had removed president number two and several faculty members; that it had already, before my arrival or election, filled the vacancies; that it had already (September 1) expended all the state money available for maintenance for that fiscal year up till the following April 1. After this and a somewhat fuller (but none the brighter) revelation of the situation as they saw it, they commended the infant college to my care and graciously gave me the full authority to act in their capacity during their absence and informed me that they would hold me responsible for results, after which they took the evening train for their distant homes.

TWO WEEKS LATER, ON THE FIRST DAY OF HIS FIRST school year, Bryan got a telephone call from Regent Stearns, who got right to the point: How many students?

Twenty-three, said Bryan.

"What did you say?" said Stearns. "There is something the matter with this phone. (shaking it). There, I asked how many students did you enroll today?"

"As I said, Mr. Stearns, twenty-three."

"The very ____ ____! (Mr. Stearns was always very picturesque in his language).

"Yes, Mr. Stearns, that seems a small number. But it is raining today. Perhaps we will have a larger number when the sun shines."

Unfortunately, Bryan mused ruefully, the sun didn't shine.

Rain, which in normal years did not begin until October, repeatedly interrupted farmers' attempts to harvest their wheat. The rain persisted. Wheat sprouted on the stalk, and bags of grain already harvested and waiting in the fields burst with moisture.

Uncowed, Bryan and his faculty took stock of the situation. Of those 23 students, they temporarily enrolled three as sophomores and four as freshmen, with the rest as preparatory students. Washington state had very few high schools. Bryan and his faculty would have to prepare them for college work. By the end of the year, the college had eleven collegiate students within its ranks, and a total of 110 enrolled. With hard work and persistence (and they were "good and promising young people"), the college would graduate its first class in 1897.

BRYAN'S BRIEF, BUT SWEETLY EVOCATIVE, ACCOUNT OF his childhood makes clear the roots of his values and motivation. He was born in a one-room log house on an 80-acre farm near Bloomington, Indiana, on May 10, 1855. His parents had moved there from Ohio just a few months prior to his birth for his father to become pastor of the Presbyterian church in Bloomington.

His first recollection of school was of a large brick building a half mile from his home. "The point of remembrance was a very cold, snowy day which must have been in the winter of 1859." He arrived at school late and very cold, bundled with a woolen muffler around his neck, his feet freezing.

The teacher unbundled him and set him next to the large wood stove in the middle of the room. "The kindness of the teacher made a lasting impression on me and I have loved her ever since."

On the day of the 1860 presidential election, young Albert, as he was known in childhood, got himself in trouble for talking to a classmate during study time, unable to resist the urge to declare that his parents voted for Lincoln. Proud of his embrace of the party of Lincoln and later Teddy Roosevelt, Bryan would frequently throughout his life remind people that he was a Republican—in spite of his equally persistent insistence that academics and politics did not mix.

During the buildup toward the Civil War, his sister Lizzie and others made a U.S. flag and mounted it on a poplar pole cut by the school's "big boys." That night it was cut down by local "copperheads," a faction of Democrats who opposed the war.

Bryan worked hard on their farm, guiding a cultivator pulled by horses Jack and Julia through the large cornfield that would produce the corn that he hauled on horseback to the local grain mill.

"When old Julia died the next winter, it was a family tragedy, for that left us only with Jack, and we loved Julia whom the folks had brought from Ohio with them." Young Albert raised sheep and hogs and became adept at shearing sheep and butchering.

His work on the farm and the responsibility of taking his two sisters to their new teaching jobs at schools miles apart meant that young Albert received little schooling between 1867 and 1870.

When he was fourteen, the family moved into Bloomington. His sisters were attending college, and he started school again. In spite of being timid and shy, he was immediately befriended by the forthright Albert Woodburn, who later became a distinguished scholar of American history and with whom Bryan remained a friend for the rest of his life.

"Beginning then, I developed a thirst for education. Albert Woodburn was not much of a student—he loved play too well. But I studied, and he began to study, and we both made progress. I learned the Constitution of the United States perfectly; and began to 'see some sense' in Grammar."

In the spring of 1872 Bryan's family, in "straitened circumstances," moved back to the farm, with one horse and a cow, and he started, "with enthusiasm," to put in a crop. The next winter he started college at Indiana University, walking from the farm to school each day, and the next year he asked for a position as a school teacher—and got it. He taught again the following year and got a raise, of $0.25 a day, nearly all of which he spent on a three-year-old colt.

In 1877 he re-entered college and continued until he finished, the following year, receiving a degree in classics. His parents had hoped that all three sons would become preachers. However, William followed the path Albert had chosen and eventually became president of Indiana University. The youngest, Joseph—who was thought to love a "good time" too much to show promise as a preacher—did fulfill their wishes.

Although the pastor of Bryan's church assured Albert that he might make a good preacher, he was burdened by "bashfulness." "I was especially awkward and unused to social ways."

Nevertheless, he began to realize he was a fair speaker and scholar and "began to hope that I would be able to do something worth while."

The next step toward doing something worthwhile was offered him in the form of becoming superintendent of the Grayville, Illinois, schools. In 1881, he married Harriet "Hattie" E. Williams, of Grayville. They would have four children: Bertha, Arthur, Eliza, and Gertrude.

They remained in Grayville until 1882, when he was offered a professorship in Latin and Greek at Vincennes University. He was soon after made president, in which position he remained until he moved west to become president of the fledgling Washington Agricultural College and School of Science.

Twenty years after Bryan accepted the challenge of leading a new college, the 1913 *Chinook*, the college yearbook, opened with a lengthy homage to Bryan's legacy. In part it offered this assessment:

> We realize full well that the growth, the development of the State
> College, has not been due to the natural outgrowth of the economic
> conditions of Washington, but rather that the magnificent build-
> ings, the atmosphere of learning, the joys, the hopes, the memories,
> all, in fact, that make the institution dear to our hearts, have been
> brought about chiefly through the efforts of one man—Enoch Albert
> Bryan—that but for his untiring and persistent work the State College
> would stand today as it did fifteen or twenty years ago, an agricultural
> college in embryo, without organization, without equipment, and
> without support.

Over those 20 years and the remaining two years of his tenure, Bryan built the physical plant of the college from the two buildings he inherited to 18, a faculty from 10 to 142, and a student enrollment from that initial 23 to 1,778. When he retired, the college was managing five experiment stations and an extension service in every one of the state's 39 counties. He established the various departments in agriculture and engineering and established courses in English, foreign languages, music, fine arts, mining, the sciences, veterinary medicine, pharmacy, military science, physical education, home economics, business administration, history, sociology, and education.

Obviously, the accomplishments were not his alone. But the *Chinook* paean was pretty accurate. Besides sheer persistence and gumption, one thing that made it all possible is that Bryan had a remarkable talent not only for hiring well, but for convincing candidates that accepting a position at such a tenuous venue with so little pay and security must somehow be worth it.

BY THE END OF THE 1895 LEGISLATIVE SESSION, TWO
years into the college's reorganization, Bryan was expressing cautious
optimism: "The college was now about to enter upon a better period.
Within a month after the adjournment of the legislature, plans had
been adopted for the construction of the new hall for women." In addition, the campus got a new dairy manufacturing plant, a heating and
lighting plant—and much more, including the furnishing of the new
administration building. And new tennis courts.

"The great day of the closing year, however," wrote Bryan, "was to
be the dedication of the Administration building," on June 26, 1895.
The building, now Thompson Hall, was begun in 1893 and finished in
the fall of 1894. It is built of brick made of clay quarried from a pit just
back of the current Stevens Hall and set on a basement story of granite.

> One can readily understand how, after a long and bitter struggle, we
> were disposed to make as much as possible of the occasion. The most
> important building of the institution was to be dedicated; the college
> had just come through the legislative session triumphantly; the foun-
> dation of Stevens hall was already laid; important minor buildings
> were under way. The spirit of permanence with a feeling of optimism,
> prevailed throughout the college circle and the community, and the
> feeling was that the most should be made of it.

And quite an occasion it was. As there were as yet no seniors to
graduate, the occasion would be a substitute for commencement.

Downtown, a crowd of regents, officers of the college, military
cadets, the Colfax military band, officers of the city, the Pullman Lodge
Independent Order Odd Fellows, citizens, Uniformed Rank Knights of
Pythias, Pullman Camp 110 Woodmen of the World, all organized for
a grand march to campus.

In his dedicatory address, President Bryan celebrated the evolution
of modern education.

"Were I asked wherein has come about the greatest change I should
answer, in the attitude of man toward the material world—in the study
of what by common consent we have come to call 'science.'"

(top) An early view of the campus, 1900.
Historic WSU Photographs Collection, pc004b14. WSU MASC.

(bottom) The campus in 1911, photography by Robert Burns.
Ivan Shirrod Images Collection, pc117_022. WSU MASC.

THE LAND-GRANT COLLEGES OF THE UNITED STATES
owe their existence, and mission, to the Morrill Act of 1862. Introduced
to Congress by Justin Morrill of Vermont, the act gave federal lands to
the states, with which they would fund designated land-grant institutions. The mission of these institutions was to focus on the teaching of
practical agriculture, science, military science, and engineering.

The mission of the land-grants was expanded by the Hatch Act of 1887, which provided funding for agricultural experiment stations directed by each state's land-grant college. The Smith-Lever Act of 1914 created cooperative extension services.

Bryan's homage in the *Historical Sketch* to Justin Morrill describes well his own sentiment toward education and, indeed, his vision: "Like all of his kind he was an admirer—almost a worshipper of the college and of college education. 'If the college can do so much for men in the Law, in the Ministry and Medicine—for men in the Learned Professions—why can it not, with proper modification of means and methods and ends, do much for the industrial classes?' "

Even by 1893, the interpretation of the relationship amongst science, agriculture, and the liberal arts (the Morrill Act stressed that its mandate did not exclude "classical" studies) was still evolving, and Bryan became known as one of the land-grant idea's prominent intellectual proponents. He chided early attempts at implementing the land-grant idea for an aversion to science. "Others were afraid to plunge into science and technology as related to life's industries lest someone of their students might escape from the shop or the farm. The professor of Chemistry and Botany knew that his pure science was mysteriously related to agriculture and mechanic arts but he was fearful lest its real educational value might be contaminated by a utilitarian end."

It was thus Bryan's mission to correct these misconceptions.

From the beginning, Bryan was certain what an agricultural school should be. It should include not only science, but music. And foreign languages.

As the college developed, every student, no matter what their major, studied chemistry, American and European history, mathematics, English literature, and two foreign languages.

Bryan was adamant that science was the key to agriculture. But he was as lyrical in his analysis as doctrinaire. In a speech to the Association of Land-Grant Colleges and Universities in 1898, he said, "Slowly the notion was forming that the mind grows by what it feeds upon, and that it feeds upon the multitude of sensations which come flocking inward through the open windows of all the senses; that the blue-bird's wing and the silver sheen of the speckled trout meet with a corresponding somewhat in the human mind just as surely as does the epigram of Plato; that truth and beauty lie no more deeply concealed in every dull clod and crawling worm of this great cosmos about us than in the mysteries of this microcosm within us."

And certainly he agreed with his fellow Hoosier farmer, Abraham Lincoln, that "no other human occupation opens so wide a field for the profitable and agreeable combination of labor with cultivated thought, as agriculture."

By 1896, "light was beginning to appear on the financial horizon throughout the state," Bryan writes in *Historical Sketch*. Spokane was showing signs of prosperity, due mainly to mining. The price of wheat had inched up, and "the spirit of optimism began to pervade the entire community. But it was also the worst of times. Populists were on the rise in Washington politics, resulting in the election of John R. Rogers as governor. "Retrenchment in expenditures and reductions in salaries of employees throughout the state were demanded by the voters." Attacks on the college erupted across the state. Worse, Governor Rogers appointed two members to the Board of Regents who were completely antagonistic. Rogers later relented and indeed became a strong advocate for the college.

Nevertheless, Bryan would later call this period "The most serious crisis in the affairs of the State College during my administration."

In spite of the turbulent background, Bryan and his inaugural crop of seniors celebrated the college's first commencement in June 1897. "Eight members of the class were advanced to degrees—three in engineering, one in biology, two in economics and two in English—quite typical of the work of the college with the exception of agriculture. Professors Spillman and Balmer, of the departments of agriculture and horticulture, had entered the faculty a year later than the other members."

Faculty had approved degrees of bachelor of science in civil and mechanical engineering, geology, chemistry, agriculture, horticulture, botany, economic science, and history, as well as bachelor of letters degrees in English and modern languages. Graduates were also required to write a rigorous senior thesis.

Commencement the following year saw the college's first agricultural major, as well as the first two graduate students and the graduation of the first class, of four students, in pharmacy.

During the 1899 session of the legislature, a name change for the college was first proposed. Bryan and his allies believed that the current name, The Agricultural College, Experiment Station, and School of Science of the State of Washington, was both cumbersome and misleading. Bryan was concerned that the name was a "hindrance to the fulfillment of the very functions of the college prescribed by both state and national law. People would persist in a wholly erroneous interpretation of the functions of the college, thinking that it was confined to instruction in farming and having a total misconception as to what instruction in agriculture involved."

The request "brought violent attacks from various sources," wrote Bryan, "chiefly from those who were out of sympathy with its purposes or ignorant of the theory and practice of the land grant colleges and universities."

The attempts to change the name would continue for several more years. Finally, the 1905 legislature approved a bill introduced by Rep. E. E. Smith of Whitman County to change the college's name to State College of Washington, which, Bryan believed, better reflected the true nature of the college.

"THE ACADEMIC YEAR 1898–9, THE SIXTH FROM ITS beginning, marks the close of the period of reorganization. From that date forward the college was a going concern, its principal lines clearly marked out, it characteristics determined, the attacks on its autonomy plainly futile." Ferry Hall and Science Hall were erected. Many additions were made to the faculty.

By the college's fourth commencement, in June 1900, 386 students were enrolled, up from 300 the previous year. Fourteen bachelor's degrees were awarded, as were two pharmacy degrees. But even more significant was the dedication of Science Hall, the older part of the current location of the Edward R. Murrow College of Communication.

In his dedication, Bryan envisioned the building as a "temple to science," repeating his belief that science would solve humanity's problems, and that "every building erected in the name of an advancing humanity is a sacred building."

Besides offering space for the biological sciences and geology and, temporarily, agriculture, horticulture, and veterinary sciences, Science Hall would also house the museum.

Rooms were allotted for agriculture, horticulture and forestry, veterinary science, zoology, ethnology, and geology. An herbarium was also located near the botanical laboratory as a working collection. The museum, writes Bryan, was much visited.

Notably, the new Science Hall, at least temporarily, also provided rooms for the Columbian, Washington, and Websterian literary societies.

Besides the day-to-day hard work—physically, administratively, and politically—of building a college from the ground up, Bryan was always assiduous about reserving time for reflection and interaction. In the case of Science Hall, one is struck by the intellectual opportunity offered by the mingling of disciplines.

But the impact of Science Hall was also immediate: "Under the inspiration of the larger space afforded by Science Hall and the increased equipment, the biological sciences and agricultural courses made a quick response and the number of students in these departments increased accordingly."

BRYAN'S GRANDDAUGHTER, HARRIET ALEXANDER, remembers sitting on her grandfather's lap long after his retirement as president. She muses on the traits that made him both a memorable and loving grandfather and that reflect his ability and accomplishments as a college president. He would read to her from his library. "He was obviously very literate," she says.

"He had a tremendous sneeze," she recalls with a laugh. Also, he was "definitely a man who enjoyed his power."

Bryan's sneeze is never mentioned elsewhere, but his appreciation of power certainly permeates his writing. But power in the sense that he was well aware of being the college's creator and enabler, with all of the accompanying responsibility.

That power only occasionally met resistance.

Besides being president of the college, Bryan was also director of the experiment station. Although this dual role was the exception among land-grants, Bryan defended it as "having been of vital importance to the very existence of the institution during its early years."

Further, "It was also a necessary measure of economy. In general it had thus far proved satisfactory to all concerned."

But by 1901 the stresses and responsibilities accompanying the rapidly growing college and their demand on the presidential role were increasingly detracting from the directorship, creating what Bryan called centrifugal in place of centripetal stress.

Undoubtedly, Bryan acknowledged, "there was a feeling on the part of some members of the experimental staff that the time was now approaching when the station should have a separate director who should devote his entire time to it."

He also acknowledged that at least some members of the experiment station felt the director should have some training in the sciences he was directing. After all, Bryan's education was in classics.

Bryan was a bit prickly about this. "I had perhaps as clear a conception of scientific experimentation and was capable of as good an understanding of proposed projects of investigation as the members of my staff and had the added merit of being free from bias."

While staff members' expertise was in the sciences, his expertise was in administration. He was largely justified in his defense, for he was, in spite of his education, remarkably well-versed in the sciences and conversant with the work of the scientists he oversaw.

The staff's discontent led finally to a meeting between Bryan and representatives, the crux of the meeting being the question of control.

"President Bryan," said one, "if the opinion of all the members of the staff on an important question were on one side and your opinion were on the other, which would prevail and decide the matter?"

"Mine," said Bryan, with no hesitation.

He went on to assure them that such a case would never happen, as they were all reasonable men, and "our judgement is based on the same set of facts."

Bryan assures us that all ended well. He would finally resign as director six years later, in 1907.

Bryan's exertion of power, or rather of control, was more blatant with the students, who in spite of his strong ruling philosophy of *in loco parentis*, by all appearances adored him. That is not to say they didn't rebel. But in the end, the "benevolent" part of benevolent despot held sway.

According to student life historian William Stimson, students referred to Bryan as "prexie," and the campus was "just a big student family with teachers as foster parents." This relationship was undoubtedly more exaggerated because in the earlier years, many of the student body were younger preparatory students.

Although faculty served as Bryan's parental proxies, in the end he took responsibility in the most direct way. According to George Frykman's centennial history, in October 1895, Bryan wrote letters to three parents "reporting with 'deep regret' that he had suspended their sons for becoming drunk in Moscow and then visiting houses of ill-fame there and in Pullman."

"It is absolutely necessary," wrote Bryan, "where a large number of young men are committed to our care to use every precaution to prevent debauchery and to ensure good conduct."

On the more benevolent side, when students complained about the quality of dining hall food, he sent the dining steward his recommended changes to the menu.

President Bryan serving students, 1913.
*Historic WSU Photographs Collection, pc004b35fbryan_*
bryancday1913. WSU MASC.

BRYAN'S REPUTATION MUST SURELY OWE AT LEAST A
partial debt to historical distance, as well as to the fact that much of his
presidential narrative was related by himself, through *Historical Sketch*
and numerous other writings. Still, his diligence, character, and accomplishment deserve continued veneration.

There is no glossing over the difficulties of starting the college, rang-
ing from simple lack of funding to outright animosity from a range of
critics, from supporters of the University of Washington who accused
the upstart college of wanting to be a university also, to local farmers
and businessmen who thought the college too unconcerned with the
details of farming.

Even so, accounts of those early days are exciting and inspiring,
at times making the atmosphere on College Hill downright halcyon,

filled with the excitement of building something from the ground up, of seeing a dream come to life.

Regents' minutes illustrate the day-to-day handling of scientific developments of both regional and international significance: Publication of C. V. Piper's *Flora of Southeastern Washington and Adjacent Idaho* and his *Flora of the Northwest Coast*. Axel Melander's leave of absence to study San Jose Scale (an insect that harms agriculture, particularly fruit) at Harvard and his subsequent discovery of insect resistance to pesticides. William Spillman's inadvertent rediscovery of Mendelian genetic laws through his wheat breeding.

The Bryan years were indeed a rich and creative time. Again, he did not do it on his own. He was assisted by an engaged Board of Regents, who if not always compliant, clearly understood his vision and did their utmost to realize it. His educational ideas were implemented by a vigorously talented faculty who worked hard and long hours for measly pay. But Bryan ultimately can take credit for his clear vision and leadership.

His success can also be attributed not only to his intimate involvement in designing and managing a developing institution, but more important to the ideas upon which it was being built. He clearly understood what his faculty were doing and was conversant in their inventions and developments.

He wrote exhaustively about their ideas and his own, on subjects as diverse as educational history and philosophy and Plato's philosophy, on the swine industry and the small orchard, on soil erosion and the use of mules on the Palouse, on the difference between Dante's and Milton's hells.

In 1904 Bryan retired from teaching, though there is some indication that he had attempted to give up his teaching responsibilities three years earlier. Nevertheless, one wonders at his ability to balance a heavy teaching load with the directorship of the Experiment Station and the presidency! For the first ten years of his presidency he had been teaching medieval history, modern history of Europe and the United States, English and American constitutional history, political economy, and labor history. He also chaired the Department of Economic Science and History.

"I had always enjoyed teaching thoroughly," he writes, "and did not for many years feel the strain of long hours and intensive work.

"Fortunately, I possessed the faculty of the quick discharge of any subject in hand and quick attention to the next, whether these subjects related to teaching, executive duties, college discipline, or the general situation."

Nevertheless, "it was indeed a joy" to turn over the chairmanship and further teaching to W. G. Beach.

Bryan expresses both his sense of control and the fairness of his analysis in reflecting on the character of Beach. According to Bryan, Beach was widely known to have "liberal" views. "While he could not properly be described as a Socialist, he had some tendencies in common with those who held that point of view."

Bryan, on the other hand, was widely known to be "pretty conservative in the interpretation of economic, social and political organization and phenomena."

According to Bryan, it was Beach who expressed concern over their political differences. "I promptly replied that I not only wished very much that he would accept the appointment but that I had not the slightest hesitancy in asking him to do so."

"You will teach your students how to think and find the truth," he instructed Beach, "and will be concerned with that chiefly and with the methods of research, and I am glad to entrust to you the department which I deem so highly important to the college and to the public welfare."

IN 1905, THE REGENTS APPROVED A THREE-YEAR SCHOOL of Music. Bryan asserted, "In the olden day music was deemed a vital part of education and it was looked upon not as 'an accomplishment' but as an essential element in the education of the human soul."

From the beginning, Bryan deemed music essential.

"What! Music in an agricultural college?" exclaimed one of the critics whose vision, as recorded by Brian, "did not rise above the pigsty and the cow barns."

"Yes," I replied, "There if anywhere. If we were in Boston we would not need a music department. Here we cannot do without it."

Bryan's love of music was hardly isolated. In 1906, a group of area private citizens built a conservatory and leased it to the college.

Bryan described the years 1906–7 as the close of a second "period of development." "The college had by this time acquired a bulk and solidarity which no mere statistics can properly present." His optimism was undoubtedly enhanced by the passage of the Adams Act of 1906, which in addition to the Hatch Act of 1887 greatly increased research possibilities.

But more significant was the sense of continuity. He went on to compare Washington State College to other regional institutions in terms of solidity and continuity.

"In the fourteen years since the reorganization of the college there had been six presidents or acting presidents in the University of Washington, at least four in the University of Oregon and four in the University of Idaho."

In contrast, he writes, with no attempt at false humility, Washington State College had one. Perhaps even more significant was the number of faculty who had stuck with the developing college over that period.

IN 1907 BRYAN CONTRACTED TYPHOID FEVER, WHICH left him completely debilitated. The regents insisted he take a three-month leave of absence to recuperate. This would be his first time off from the presidency.

The students welcome President Bryan upon his return from
Europe, 1908. Bryan sits at right in the wagon being pulled by the
students. *Historic WSU Photographs Collection, pc004b35fbryan_
bryanreturns1908. WSU MASC.*

He took advantage of this to travel in Europe, visiting Italy, France,
and England.

When he returned, he was met at the train station in Pullman by a
"shouting mass of students." He was placed in a buggy, and the students
pulled him up the hill to his house—"a royal welcome home which I by
no means deserved but which made my return to my beloved college a
very happy one."

He also returned to welcome appropriations from the legislature
for six buildings, including a new library and assembly hall (soon to be
named Bryan Hall), a recitation building (College Hall), and a domestic
economy building (Van Doren)—plus generous maintenance funds.

"Six important buildings! A goodly sum for maintenance! Was it
any wonder that the hearts of the college people should rejoice!" (These
may be the only exclamation marks in his entire *Historical Sketch*.)

In his annual report for the April 1910 regents' meeting, Bryan wrote,
"I do not think there has been a time in the history of the college when

we have been blest with more loyal and competent men at the head of several departments than at the present time." In *Historical Sketch* he reflects that the same could have been said about the entire faculty.

At the same time, he was exhausted and determined to resign. "I was tired, mentally and physically, and perceived that my wife also was much in need of release from the long strain of responsibility which she had cheerfully borne with admirable fortitude for some seventeen long years."

Except for the three months of recuperation from typhoid, he had had no vacation since arriving in Pullman in 1893. Neither had he fully recovered his strength from his illness. The regents declined to act immediately on his resignation, and the news spread across the state.

Strong protests erupted, from alumni, from citizens, from students. None would consider letting President Bryan resign, and he withdrew his request in exchange for a leave of absence.

At the end of the 1910 commencement exercises, R. C. McCroskey, chairman of the board, announced that President Bryan had withdrawn his resignation.

"A wild demonstration followed," writes Bryan, "in which my wife shared with me in witnessing the evidence of loyalty and affection of students, alumni and faculty."

Bryan was granted a leave of absence from April 15, 1911, until February 17, 1912, during which he planned another trip to Europe. However, he delayed his family's departure until fall, meanwhile directing the policy of the institution from the family's residence, in spite of the entirely capable direction of vice-president O. L. Waller.

The family's European trip was somewhat eclipsed by his daughters' contraction of typhoid, from which they quickly recovered. Bryan was pleased with a trip to the Agricultural College at Wye, where he observed much evidence of English adaptation of Pacific Northwest horticultural principles. Also, on a visit to a lab exploring principles of Mendel's law at Cambridge University, he saw photographs of studies in wheat hybridizing. "Why that looks like Professor Spillman's work," he exclaimed. Indeed it was, his guide assured him, which pleased him greatly.

Upon his return from Europe, Bryan found signs of some disturbance, created no doubt by his absence and expectations that he might resign. Otherwise, he continued as he had before, planning, envisioning, leading the steadily growing college. For the next three years, that is.

"Near the beginning of the year 1915 I determined to resign the presidency of the college and retire from educational work on January 1, 1916. I was in excellent health and happy in the consciousness of the sound and prosperous condition of the college. . . . There was not a cloud in the sky and I felt sure that, with sufficient time to seek a new president, the institution would go forward without a jar."

Naturally the board resisted his wishes, urging him to reconsider and offering more salary to stay on. But this time Bryan was adamant. He had done what he could do. He had done well. And it was time to turn over the helm.

"After the announcement had been made," he writes, "the work of the college went forward quite as usual, and as though it would continue thus forever."

(above) President Bryan on WSC Foundation Day, March 28, 1911. Governor Lister sits at right in the car, while Osmar L. Waller (after whom Waller Hall is named) stands beside the vehicle. *Historic WSU Photographs Collection, pc004b35fbryan_86-0032. WSU MASC.*

(right) Historic WSU Photographs Collection, pc004b35fbryan_86-0010. WSU MASC.

As Bryan remarked to the Board of Regents at his last meeting, "I clearly perceive that it is utterly impossible for the State College to be separated from me, or me from it. It is like the family tie which no distance breaks. The legal and official relations cease, but there are relations deeper which can never cease. And to me this fact is a source of comfort and happiness."

Following six years in Boise as Commissioner of Education for the State of Idaho, Bryan returned to Washington State College as a research professor of economics and economic history. In 1937 he was named president emeritus. Besides *Historical Sketch* and extensive essays on many subjects, he was author of *The Mark in Europe and America* and *Occident Meets Orient*. He died in 1941 and is buried at the Fairmount Cemetery in Pullman next to his beloved wife Hattie and daughter Bertha.

RESEARCH NOTES

The main source for this essay was Bryan's *Historical Sketch of the State College of Washington 1890–1925* (Alumni and the Associated Students, 1928). Beyond the obvious advantage of such a history written by the protagonist, *Historical Sketch* provides continuous insights, anecdotes, and historical details that make for absorbing reading. Also invaluable was the extensive section on the Bryan years in George Frykman's *Creating the People's University: Washington State University, 1890–1990* (Washington State University Press, 1990). The regents' minutes, for which Bryan was secretary, give a timely and often engaging narrative of academic and administrative proceedings.

Finally, providing texture, if you will, and creating a fascinating self-portrait, was Bryan's voluminous collected writing. Manuscripts, Archives, and Special Collections in the WSU library hold 800 items written by Bryan, not including collected personal correspondence. The subjects of these writings vary wildly, from the expected extensive writings on economics, his primary academic discipline, to principles of livestock judging, educational philosophy, the small orchard, clog dancing, Ralph Waldo Emerson, and personal character.

Regardless of topic, Bryan was a fine and engaging writer, often an eloquent one, and will reward any reader interested in the founding and growth of Washington State College and the creative force behind it.

Ernest O. Holland
1916–1945

BY TREVOR JAMES BOND

B RIEFLY WAKING FROM A COMA, ERNEST O. Holland, president emeritus of Washington State College, uttered his final words to his sister Edith Gifford: "Do you love Washington State College as I do?" So passed one of WSU's most devoted administrators. Perhaps best remembered today by the research library on the Pullman campus that bears his name, Holland was Washington State University's longest serving president (1916–1945).

When Holland first arrived in Pullman, he addressed students and townspeople in the Bryan Hall auditorium telling the crowd of 1,300 that his "experience in educational matters has all been with institutions that had previously gone wrong, but now I have affiliated with one that has gone right." Afterward he and retiring president, Dr. E. A. Bryan, received tremendous ovations. Holland exited the auditorium and crossed the hall to the library where he shook hands with the entire audience as a long line slowly filed past. This goodwill that Holland received from the students, faculty, and regents would help him in the challenges he soon would face.

Holland's presidency included some of the most difficult events ever confronted by a college administrator: the prospect of losing degree offerings to a rival university, quarantining campus during the 1918 influenza pandemic, major budget cuts and mandatory reductions in salaries during the Great Depression, and managing WSC through two world wars. Holland met these challenges with his own blend of decisive leadership, a careful eye on the budget, and an inexhaustible work ethic. When Holland began his tenure, WSC had 140 faculty and 1,778 students. Toward the end of Holland's administration, the campus had more than quadrupled to 750 faculty and 4,274 students. Beyond increasing the size of WSC, Holland steered the institution from a small land-grant college to a comprehensive university.

Holland was a hands-on leader. He knew the minute details of all aspects of college administration. His biographer, William Landeen, called him a "personal" president. This style of management, best suited to a small college, became harder for Holland to maintain as WSC grew. Indeed, Holland was the last president to be involved in all aspects of administration. His successors adopted a more executive style and dele-gated responsibilities to other administrators. Holland kept a sharp eye on everything happening on campus, including the welfare of individual students. Ed Goldsworthy serves as an example. Ed did not connect with his roommate on arrival at WSC and was feeling isolated on campus. His father, who served on the appropriations committee of the state legislature, wanted his son to live in the dorms for a year to adjust to his academic responsibilities before joining a fraternity. Young Goldsworthy received a message to report to President Holland, who questioned him on how he was doing and, after receiving a guarded response, asked if he was lonesome. Goldsworthy admitted as much, and Holland said, "Would you feel more at home and feel better if you were living in a fraternity?" Goldsworthy replied, "Well, I really would." So Holland said, "Well, I'll get you cleared to move in." Ed Goldsworthy recalled, "I don't know whether my father contacted him or whether there was some discussion or not. But for a man running the school to take that time off to call a little freshman in and talk to him about his situation, and in this case he was a pretty compassionate man." This is but one example of Holland's close attention to a student's welfare.

Holland just before the start of his administration, ca. 1914. He was forty-one years old when he accepted the presidency of WSC. Holland retained his preference for formal dress throughout his life. *Historic WSU Photographs Collection, pc004b35afHolland_ca1914portrait. WSU MASC.*

Unlike every other WSU President, Holland never married. During much of his administration he worked incessantly and at all hours, personally responding to vast numbers of letters that arrived daily. This work ethic eventually ruined his health. He was an astute politician and kept his job through partisan governorships and challenging budget years. He had the complete support of WSC's regents and the respect of the student body. However, in the last decade of his administration, the faculty and the students at times chaffed under Holland's close watch.

Born in Bennington, Indiana, February 4, 1874, Holland grew up in a well-educated family, the son of a physician. Holland earned his bachelor's degree at Indiana University and his doctorate from Columbia University. At Columbia Holland studied under John Dewey and Henry Suzzallo, later president of the University of Washington. Holland and Suzzallo became friends and roommates, and Holland was the best man at Henry Suzzallo's wedding in Chicago in 1912.

After graduating from Columbia in 1911, Holland received several job offers. He declined a faculty position at Stanford University and the superintendency of the Portland, Oregon, school district. Instead, he became the superintendent of schools for Louisville, Kentucky, where he instituted major reforms and quickly gained a reputation as a capable school administrator. In the views of his contemporaries, Holland found a school system in poor condition and turned it into a model district with increased state funding. Holland's success in Louisville made him an attractive candidate for other administrative positions.

WHEN THE PRESIDENCIES OF THE UNIVERSITY OF Washington and Washington State College (WSC) opened, William Foster, president of Reed College and a former classmate and friend of Holland's from Columbia University, recommended Holland for both positions. Holland wrote to Foster that he thought his chances for the University of Washington's presidency slim, "since I am unmarried and not at present engaged in college work."

IN 1915 THE UNIVERSITY OF WASHINGTON PRESIDENCY went to Holland's friend and former mentor Henry Suzzallo. Still, a secretive lobbying effort to hire Holland for the WSC presidency was underway. The brother of WSC President Enoch Bryan, William Lowe Bryan, president of Indiana University, strongly recommended Holland, noting in a letter that Holland was not a church member, but wherever he lived he "identified himself with some church work." Holland told William Bryan that he "expect[ed] to be married within two years, possibly within a year and a half." Holland continued: "if I were to accept a college presidency, it is understood that Father and Mother" would "live with me until my marriage."

Henry Suzzallo and William Foster also advocated for Holland for the Washington State College position. On July 8, 1915, Suzzallo wrote to E. T. Coman, president of the WSC regents, "I think that he [Holland] is one of the best executive officers I have ever known." Suzzallo continued, "Dr. Holland will make a success of any institution that he heads. He is one of the rare combinations of tact and forcefulness that I have ever known." Holland "never vacillates, yet he never bullies, and seldom offends even those who may be in opposition."

On October 15, 1915, the WSC Board of Regents offered Holland the presidency, succeeding Enoch Bryan. In the statement announcing Holland's hiring, the regents described the new president as "young in years but well matured in educational experience and achievement. He has made a lifelong study of problems of efficiency as connected with educational administration." Holland was 41 as he began his presidency and received a total annual salary of $12,000. The search process was a secretive affair with the regents relying on the advice of President Bryan, his brother, and regional leaders, such as Suzzallo, but without any WSC faculty or student input.

Holland began his duties at an exciting moment for WSC. The football team had just won the Rose Bowl, defeating Brown University 14–0. Holland delayed his arrival in Pullman to allow the football team to return in celebration. In his inaugural address in January 1916, Holland articulated his vision of WSC as a land-grant college with strengths in the sciences and humanities. According to Holland, "There should be in every school of science and technology a strong faculty, teaching the humanities—English literature, history, economics and foreign languages." Holland continued, "Without such a faculty the students would be robbed of much of their heritage and prevented from taking their rightful places as educated citizens in the practical world of affairs." Holland wanted the graduates of WSC to become engaged citizens. He argued, "college graduates should be interested, vitally interested, in the community, —its religious life, its schools, its local government, and in all things looking toward the building of the community and the state."

In a display of friendship and cooperation at the start of the Holland's tenure, University of Washington President Henry Suzzallo and his wife, Edith, visited Pullman, where Suzzallo spoke and attended a faculty reception. Holland and Suzzallo's warm friendship and mutual support, however, quickly became strained over a brewing fight about university and college course offerings. At issue was a concern voiced in the state legislature over the duplication of courses and degrees, and too much state spending on higher education. The dispute over course offerings became a major concern for Holland and WSC, as it threatened to reduce the range of degrees offered and hinder future growth.

Suzzallo took the position that the University of Washington should solely offer the majority of college and graduate degrees. On June 22, 1915, Suzzallo wrote to Holland with the following argument: "I am unwilling to make a single compromise that interferes with efficiency and economy," explaining that WSC, "ought, if its funds are devoted for that purpose, be the greatest school of agriculture in the world." For his part, Holland wanted more for WSC than to be the "greatest school of agriculture." In December Holland wrote to his friend in an effort to reconcile: "I think it will not be long before some solution can be found for most of our difficulties. What is needed is frankness of speech and liberality of spirit." Holland continued, "A state the size of Washington. . . . I believe ought to present enough education problems to keep us busy with cooperative work rather than quarreling. I am sending you a large olive branch with this letter." Reconciliation was not forthcoming.

In 1916 Suzzallo proposed ending WSC's schools of architecture and pharmacy, along with its graduate programs, including engineering. Holland and the WSC regents, alumni, and supporters lobbied against the University of Washington. The debate came to a conclusion in the 1917 Washington Legislative session. After more than a year of reports, arguments in the press, and the lobbying of politicians, Governor Lister convened a meeting that resulted in a compromise bill agreed to by Suzzallo and Holland. The legislation, "Regulation of Instruction in State University, College, and Normal Schools," signed into law on February 10, 1917, defined the roles and responsibilities around the curriculum between the University of Washington, Washington State College, and the other Normal Schools (teacher colleges that would become Western, Central, and Eastern Washington Universities).

According to the new law, WSC and UW equally shared undergraduate degrees in the sciences, liberal arts, home economics, pharmacy, mining, and all engineering fields except marine and aeronautical. WSC also had equal right to train high school teachers and school administrators. WSC received exclusive right to develop agriculture, veterinary science, agricultural economics, and rural sociology degrees, while UW held full degree-granting privileges over architecture, law, human medicine (not yet offered), forestry, fisheries, commerce, journalism, library training, and marine and aeronautical engineering. The rivalry over course offerings has never disappeared. Exactly a century later it took an intense lobbying effort by then WSU President Elson S. Floyd to change the Washington state constitution in 2015 to allow WSU to open its own medical school, a move opposed by the University of Washington.

Since neither institution offered many graduate programs in 1917, the legislation stated that after a "degree granting privilege" in a particular major was established, it would also establish "the right to offer and teach graduate work." To formalize graduate studies at WSC in 1922, Holland organized the Graduate School and appointed C.C. Todd, professor of chemistry, as dean. To encourage faculty and student research, twelve faculty formed a research council. With the enthusiastic support of Holland, this research council grew to include fifty-three faculty and graduate students.

The debate with Suzzallo revealed Holland's political skills as he worked closely with the WSC regents and politicians across the state. Drawing on carefully gathered information, Holland made a persuasive case for the legitimacy of WSC and the need for the state to offer degrees at multiple institutions. The stakes were high for WSC; if Holland had not prevailed at the start of his tenure, WSC would have offered many fewer areas of study. The episode also instilled in Holland a deep and lasting concern for the college.

Holland's political skills allowed him to outlast Governors Hart and Hartley, defeated in 1924 and 1932. Henry Suzzallo was not so lucky.

Holland and the Board of Regents, 1933. From left to right: Holland, Davis, Kimbrough, Orton, Perham, and Ritz. *Historic WSU Photographs Collection, pc004b37fgroup. WSU MASC.*

He got into a dispute with Hartley after the governor replaced the UW regents, and Hartley responded to Suzzallo's comments in the press by firing the popular UW president in 1926. Holland also had a close call with the election of Governor Martin, who considered changing the leadership of WSC, but Governor Martin met such united opposition to replacing Holland that he relented and even became a strong supporter. According to Holland's biographer Landeen, Holland was "adroit in 'sizing up' situations and quick to adjust his own actions to shifts in state politics." He demonstrated his leadership for WSC by strongly advocating for the value of higher education.

In a 1925 address at Reed College entitled the "Business of Education," Holland compared the amount the United States spent on education with other luxury goods. According to Holland, Americans devoted roughly $300 million each year to maintain public and private colleges and universities. Holland noted that the country spent $200 million more than that for jewelry and seven times the costs of all of higher education on tobacco products. Holland made it clear that education was not exempt from wasteful extravagance when he asserted, "I may add that if any money is wasted in the great cause of higher education, that waste also deserves the severest condemnation." Holland continued on a hopeful note: "Assuredly we have no cause to be discouraged at the outlook for higher education in America. The doors of our institutions of higher learning should continue to open wisely for competent and worthy young men and women who desire to continue their education and prepare for lives of usefulness." This speech reflects Holland's views on the importance of education and providing a quality education economically.

Holland's deep commitment to funding education never translated into extravagance. Within the first three months of his administration, Holland addressed his first major budget challenge. WSC's two-year departmental operating budget of $92,000 was far overspent with $80,000 of the first year's budget already allocated to salary increases, new positions, repairs, and other items, leaving only $12,000 for the second year. Holland immediately identified $100,000 in cuts across the college to bring the second year's spending in line. He trimmed the spending of all departments, laid off staff for the summer, and left positions open. For Holland, economy and efficiency became his guiding principles. His extremely careful management of WSC resources positioned him for dealing with the crisis of the coming Great Depression. The unpredictable funding for WSC from the state legislature made Holland extremely conservative about spending money. He insisted on the tightest economies, fought to keep salaries low, resisted a retirement pension system for college faculty and staff, and refused state funds for activities such as student recruitment and faculty travel.

On June 12, 1917, President Holland initiated a reorganization of WSC. Under President Bryan, the chairs or heads of twenty-one departments had reported directly to the president. Replacing this unwieldy structure, Holland created five colleges (agriculture, home economics, mechanic arts and engineering, sciences and arts, and veterinary science) and four schools (mines, music and applied design, education, and pharmacy), with deans as administrative heads. This dramatic reorganization, which he made without consulting the faculty as a body, proved a key step toward eventual university status. It mirrored national trends and the structure of academic colleges overseen by administrative deans that continues to this day.

In 1918 the campus faced a major health crisis. In early October soldiers coming to campus for training prior to deployment in World War I brought a virulent and deadly strain of influenza. The virus, combined with unseasonably cold weather and hastily constructed quarters for the soldiers, proved deadly. By October 7, with twenty-five reported cases, Holland cancelled classes and closed public places on campus. The gymnasium became a temporary hospital as cases of the flu grew. Weeks later eleven soldiers had died and campus officials moved to quarantine campus. Concerned parents wrote to President Holland begging to come retrieve their children. The campus mobilized, particularly the Home Economics program, whose faculty and students cooked hundreds of meals for the sickened students. The number of cases on campus and throughout Pullman grew to nearly six hundred. Thankfully by mid-November the flu had passed, but not before fifty deaths were reported (eight civilian, forty-two student army training corps cadets). No WSC students perished.

Holland kept a close watch on campus and sought to create a healthy atmosphere. He forbade smoking and consuming alcohol on campus. Faculty member Mary Johnson recalled that the male faculty skirted the no smoking rule by hiding behind buildings or smoking in other discreet locations, but one female faculty member openly smoked outside. Holland addressed this violation personally and called all women faculty to his office. According to Professor Johnson, Holland told the following story: "Now, I used to drink a little beer when I was superintendent of schools in Louisville, Kentucky. But one day, one of the parents came to me and said, 'Do you think you are setting a very good

W.S.C. and Yale stand shoulder to shoulder.

Holland and William Howard Taft, on the WSC campus in 1920. Former President Taft was at this time a professor of law at Yale University, but would become Chief Justice of the U.S. Supreme Court the following year. *Historic WSU Photographs Collection, pc004b35a_hollandwo-misc1. WSU MASC.*

example for the boys?' so I quit drinking." When some in the meeting questioned the rule, Holland responded: "now that's your privilege, and I'll be happy to recommend you to the University of Washington or anyplace where it's considered all right. But you can't smoke here." We assume that the faculty received the message and ceased smoking in public; Holland did not vacillate in his views and was certainly willing to ask for a resignation if necessary.

Holland considered drinking a moral issue and lobbied to keep liquor stores from reopening after the repeal of prohibition in 1933. In

1936 Pullman citizens voted to permit liquor sales, much to Holland's dismay. WSC administrators continued to enforce their own alcohol ban on campus through the Holland years, though with no great success. According to the historian William Stimson, fraternity men could have whiskey delivered by a local milkman by telling him to bring a bottle of "heavy cream."

Some found charm in Holland's formal demeanor. Thelma Reuss whose husband Carl Reuss worked as sociology professor from 1937 to 1944, recalled that among her faculty friends, "everyone liked Holland and went out of their way to greet him." Holland was always "immaculately attired in attractive conservative fashion, he walked with grace and to everyone he tipped his hat and slightly drew his cane with a warm, sincere greeting." Holland and his sister Edith, who lived with him, even allowed campus organizations to hold parties and dances on the third floor of the president's mansion and "after greeting each guest, they would retire to their living quarters."

Holland closely monitored all aspects of campus administration. When he travelled or took a rare vacation, Holland expected a daily report on campus activities. Part of his reluctance to take an extended trip was the need to catch up on his missed correspondence. Holland remarked, "If I am gone four or five days I find a good deal of unanswered correspondence upon my return. Much of it is not very important, and yet it should be answered."

According to his biographer, "there was much work and little play" during the Holland years. He was "an exacting master because he himself had no concept of time." He followed a round-the-clock routine in his own work, and he expected others to keep up a similar pace. Miss Lewellen, secretary to the president, and others were constantly on call for Holland who would dictate letters and memoranda from morning till midnight. Nor were the faculty exempt. History Professor Herman Deutsch remembered that Holland "did not respect one's time, Saturdays, Sundays, and evenings" were all fair game for the president to call for a request of some sort. Only in 1941, when his health was in serious

ERNEST O. HOLLAND 75

decline, did Holland tell his brother, "I have quit working at night so to recuperate for the next day's work."

Holland kept a rigid enforcement of all aspects of economy on campus. During his administration, there was no sick leave available to campus employees. Whenever anyone was absent from the office, whatever the reason, Holland ensure that salary deductions were made. Landeen, Holland's biographer, notes "it seems a bit strange today that a secretary who had worked until midnight times without number should so suffer for a short absence, but it happened." Holland applied the rules equally to everyone.

Prior to the Great Depression, Holland had already led WSC through dramatic budget reductions. However in 1932, at the urging of the governor, Holland joined the presidents of the University of Washington and the Normal Schools in accepting a salary reduction scale. In the 1932–33 academic year, the WSC regents approved implementing the plan. Those earning $3,600 and up received a 10 percent reduction, those earning $2,600 and up a 7.5 percent cut, and those earning below $2,500 saw a 5 percent cut. Holland paid close attention to the implementation of this policy, carefully studying the impact of the reductions and ensuring complete fairness. He cut his own salary 10 percent. It is interesting to note that Holland never accepted a salary increase and that his starting pay in 1916 was higher than when he retired.

The Great Depression also dramatically impacted WSC students. Throughout the 1920s, with depressed agriculture prices, many students attended WSC with very little money. Undergraduate tuition during Holland's administration was modest, ten dollars per semester, but there were still costs associated with fees, room and board, and books. Students economized by working in kitchens and "batching it"—renting modest apartments and eating inexpensive food. One extreme example of student economy was Peter E. Kragt, who purchased lumber and built a tiny cabin on a borrowed piece of land. It was finished the day school opened. By eating lots of potatoes and avoiding groups that charged fees, Kragt lived on $140 for the entire school year. His story of survival

Holland and his sister Edith (to his left) hosting a table of WSC students in the president's house. Holland reportedly remembered the name and face of everyone with whom he had the slightest acquaintance. As Holland never married, his sister lived with him and helped host guests. *Historic WSU Photographs Collection, pco04b35afHolland_dining1. WSU MASC.*

helped him win an essay contest on the subject, "How I Economized Last Semester," sponsored by President Holland.

Holland celebrated students who struggled financially but worked their way through college. In a 1925 essay published in the *Chinook*, Holland wrote that many student leaders were forced to work as janitors or waiters in campus dining halls in order to attend WSC. According to Holland, "the student who has to earn his way is respected more highly than those who have an excess of money." He continued, "May the 'hello spirit' remain forever at the State College, because it enables the poor man or woman, coming from any obscure corner of the state, to win his way to recognition, and because it makes it impossible for the man or woman lacking in character to receive honor and hold a permanent place in the leadership of the institution."

WSC students held differing opinions on their president. Stan Berry remembered Holland as "very sedate, very sort of formal and rigid" who wore a "high white collar and black tie and was always dressed very, very neatly." But Berry continued that Holland was not as cold as his clothing might suggest. The president drove a big car around town and if he saw a student walking or waiting for the bus, Holland picked them up and would take them wherever they wanted to go and chat with them in a friendly manner. Other students found Holland too formal and his discipline committee too strict. Robert Bucklin recalled being summoned to Holland's office and receiving a lecture regarding an editorial he had written for the *Daily Evergreen*. Bucklin respected Holland but found him harsh.

In the early 1920s, students increasingly grumbled over the strict rules on campus and felt that they were arbitrarily enforced by the Dean of Women, Annie Fertig—"Dean Annie," as she was called by the students. Near the end of the term on May 4, 1936, 3,200 students participated in a strike calling for changes in rules regarding compulsory class attendance, severe penalties for non-attendance, rigid social laws, and the lack of student and faculty control of campus activities. The students demanded that they be allowed to have radios and that male students could visit sorority houses and women's dormitories. After marching and playing *The Star Spangled Banner*, twelve students met with Holland for three hours, at the end of which the twelve students agreed to call off the strike the next day as planned. But this proposal was overwhelmingly defeated by a voice vote even though Holland had agreed to their key demands: the creation of a permanent student conduct committee and that students being disciplined would be allowed to know the origin of the charges against them and be allowed student counsel for defense. Telegrams from four members of the Board of

Regents did not help matters by suggesting the students "keep their shirts on and leave if they didn't like the way the school is run."

Holland sought to avoid a general student strike, an event that would be an embarrassment to his administration and the college's reputation. Late that night Holland telephoned Robert Yothers, one of the leaders of the strike, and asked him to come to the president's mansion. When Yothers arrived, he was surprised to see the president looking so upset. Holland asked what it would take to stop the strike. Yothers responded that students would not accept a promise; the demands had to be signed. Holland seemed to find this humiliating, but sat down at the desk in his den to sign the demands. When the students continued their strike even after Holland met nearly all of their demands, he was distressed by the negative press. In an uncharacteristic action for the president, Holland retaliated against Yothers, calling him a week before graduation. Holland informed Yothers, "There's no use of you showing up to graduate. You're not going to get your diploma!" Since Yothers had enough credits for law school, he did not take the news too badly. He completed his law degree in 1941 and, after receiving credit for military service, he earned his bachelor's degree in 1957.

The mood on campus during World War II contrasted with that of the First World War, which saw large numbers of cadets coming to an unprepared campus. The lead-up to WWII was better organized and service commitments depleted campus of students. Holland followed the reports of his distinguished alumnus, Edward R. Murrow, who attended WSC from 1926 to 1930. He also directly involved himself in the issue over the internment of Japanese and Japanese American students in the West. With the onset of war against Japan, President Roosevelt issued executive order 8066 forcing Japanese and Japanese American citizens living along the west coast to move to guarded relocation centers. WSC was located outside of the relocation boundary.

In April 1942 Holland received letters from Dr. Robert Sproul of the University of California regarding a plan to have the federal government give authority and financial support to universities and colleges of the

The student strike in May 1936 called for a loosening of the strict code of conduct under Holland. *Historic WSU Photographs Collection, pc004b23strikes_1936strike. WSU MASC.*

Pacific Coast to enroll Japanese and Japanese American college students so they could continue their education. Holland supported Sproul's plan, replying that "both the faculty and students of the State College of Washington would be friendly and helpful to such students." Holland continued, "Furthermore, the people of Pullman, whom I have already consulted, would also do all they could to make these unfortunate and bewildered young men and women understand that all possible encouragement will be given to them here." At Sproul's request, Holland sent letters in support of the plan to President Roosevelt, Vice President Henry Wallace, Milton Eisenhower, head of the War Relocation Authority, and other senior officials.

Holland's assessment of the people of Pullman "doing all they could" to help the Japanese students was overly optimistic. Instead, Holland reported to the regents in May 1942 that the citizens of Pullman asked that the number of Japanese and Japanese Americans be limited. After reviewing the legality of such an action, Holland provided to the regents (and the FBI office in Spokane) lists of Japanese students enrolled in the summer session, those who had been promised admittance in September 1942, and those who had not been granted permission to enroll. After discussion, the regents determined that the enrollment of Japanese students be limited to thirty, in addition to the fourteen who were enrolled during the previous semester, and that no names be added to the list in the event that any of the fourteen should fail to return to college.

Leading up to this decision to limit the enrollment, WSC officials had corresponded with fifty-one additional students of Japanese ancestry whose names and addresses were included on a list titled "unable to consider—quota filled—etc." A number of these aspiring students had addresses at assemble centers where their families were confined on their way to the relocation centers. Only the notes of the regents meetings remain and they are sparse. It is unclear whether Holland, or others, advocated acceptance of more Japanese American students or readily accepted the quota.

On May 24, 1943, President Ernest O. Holland addressed the graduating class of the State College of Washington (WSC). Holland was in the twenty-eighth year of his presidency and nearing retirement. He exhorted the graduates to fulfill their responsibilities to society. Noting that their class size was smaller than normal, as many of their classmates had gone to war and sacrificed their lives, it was up to them to assume the responsibilities "of the period of reconstruction." Holland was hopeful that these WSC graduates would "join the silent, intelligent army of men and women who will see to it that the sacrifices of the free peoples of the world will result in economic and social stability, and in enlarged educational opportunities." These opportunities, Holland told the graduates, were for their children and their children's children.

FROM THE 1930S AND INTO HIS RETIREMENT, HOLLAND collected art, books, and manuscripts. His personal art collection included Post-Impressionist paintings that he displayed in the president's mansion. He later donated more than forty works of art to the campus. Regent Charles Orton also donated $10,000 to WSC for Holland to use to purchase works of fine art. This exemplified a commitment and interest in the arts that Holland demonstrated throughout his career. He persuaded the regents to commission WSC fine arts faculty member Worth D. Griffin to paint a series of portraits of Native Americans and pioneers. These portraits are the most significant legacy of Holland's art collecting.

During the Holland administration, campus art exhibitions were a highlight of the year. According to Worth Griffin, the campus community and Pullman residents came by the hundreds, not only to see the art, but also to interact with President Holland, who would be in a "relaxed, friendly, and approachable mood." Griffin recalled that during the lean years of the Depression Holland covered the costs for many exhibits with what he called the "Presidents Emergency Fund," an account Griffin believed was Holland's personal bank account.

TODAY, HOLLAND'S NAME IS MOST ASSOCIATED WITH the university's library. Holland wanted a magnificent new library for the campus and spent the late 1930s and the 1940s lobbying for a new building. With limited funds available and a penchant for economy at every level, Holland and Librarian W. W. Foote built library collections largely through donations. In 1941 Holland boasted to the regents, "All of us are aware of the fact that the State College of Washington has a rapidly growing and increasingly valuable library—the largest library to be found in any separate land-grant institution in the United States."

The volume of donations and the indiscriminate addition of all of them to the library's holdings put extreme pressure on library staff and quickly overwhelmed the storage capacity in Bryan Hall. For example, the

A formal portrait of Holland in 1944 near the end of his tenure. In 1941, Holland confided to his brother that he had stopped working in the evening so he could recuperate for the next day's work. *Historic WSU Photographs Collection, pc004b35a_holland1944. WSU MASC.*

library purchased 27,637 volumes in 1943 and 1944, but the total additions to the collection was 532,637 donated items. Librarian Foote stored the donated collections in basements and attics across campus. Aware of the lack of funding coming to the library from his administration, Holland created the Friends of the Library in 1938 with Spokane banker Joel Ferris as head. Holland called individual faculty members and instructed them to join. Holland also played an active role in the Friends of the Library, personally donating to the group and also directing their purchases.

Holland and the Friends of the Library had some notable acquisitions during the late 1930s and 1940s. The Inland Empire Early Birds Breakfast Club of Spokane donated $5,000 for the purchase of Spanish, French, and English books and manuscripts in Mexico and in the Central American countries. Holland sent foreign languages professor J. Horace Nunemaker to Spain and Mexico to purchase early printed books. While in Mexico Nunemaker acquired a significant body of eighteenth and nineteenth-century manuscripts related to the aristocratic Regla family in Mexico. Holland was particularly excited about the gift of 2,000 Lincoln related items collected by Dean Clark Bissett, of the University of Washington, and then purchased and donated by A. W. Witherspoon. Unfortunately, one of the highlights of the collection, a Lincoln manuscript, is a forgery.

Upon occasion, Holland spent large sums for items he particularly wanted. He acquired a twenty-eight-volume set of Meserve's *Historical Portraits*, a publication hand-produced to order that included thousands of Mathew Brady photos. Each volume was extremely expensive at $195 dollars. Holland personally purchased four of the volumes so WSC could have a complete set. To put this in some context, during the 1930s the library regularly purchased English books published in the seventeenth century for less than a dollar.

Holland was also instrumental in negotiating the gift of the library's most highly consulted manuscript collection, the papers of Lucullus V. McWhorter. McWhorter was a rancher, author, and advocate for the Yakama and Nez Perce. The collection includes priceless interviews of participants in the 1877 Nez Perce war, manuscripts of the noted author Mourning Dove, and primary sources pertaining to the native peoples of the Columbia Plateau. After McWhorter passed away, Holland promised McWhorter's son, Virgil, a WSC graduate, that the college would complete and publish McWhorter's unfinished book and also organize his papers.

During the final decade of his tenure, Holland regularly sought out collections. Holland routinely requested papers for the special collections in the library, the Treasure Room. In 1942, Holland wrote to Edward R. Murrow: "Please do not forget, Ed, that you must send us something occasionally for our Treasure Room. When this war is over, I want the material you have sent to us to be given an honored place here on the college campus. Later it can be given a special place in the new library building which I am sure will be built shortly after the close of the present world conflict." Murrow sent several transcripts and his wife Janet later donated a collection of family photographs.

Holland reluctantly retired in 1945. As Mary Johnson recalled, "Dr. Holland had been very good for his time. [WSC] needed someone of his caliber to get this young college on its way and he did that. But since he wasn't married, it was his entire life and he had the feeling, as he grew older, that he was absolutely essential to it. And that was unfortunate for him, when it came time to retire." When Holland's successor, Wilson Compton, arrived on campus, Holland had not yet moved out of the president's house or out of his office. The regents provided Holland with a house on Columbia Street, a half salary, and an office in the library in Bryan Hall where he actively collected for the library.

The WSC campus grew dramatically during Holland's presidency. During the first decade of his administration, the most acute need was for student housing. The campus added new dorms, McCroskey and Community Halls, in 1920. Without state support, campus officials worked with Pullman business leaders to form the Community Building Corporation that built Community Hall and Stimson Hall and leased them to the campus until the college could purchase them. The state legislature provided funding for new academic buildings including Troy Hall in 1926, the Home Economics Building (now known as Elmina White Honors Hall) in 1927, Chemistry Hall (now known as Fulmer Hall) in 1934, and Wegner Hall in 1941. To provide gyms and additional athletic facilities, the associated students also raised fees to fund the men's gym (Bohler) in 1925 and Hollingbery Fieldhouse in 1929.

The building most closely associated with President Holland, Holland Library, was not what Holland wanted. In 1938 Holland had plans developed for an ornate building with reading room ceilings sixty-eight feet tall (three feet taller than the University of Washington's Suzzallo Library). However, funding from the state for the new library came after Holland's retirement.

When librarian G. Donald Smith started his appointment in 1946, he found the completed library plans reflecting, in his view, an impractical structure. Instead, Smith persuaded President Compton to model the library on a functional design developed at MIT. According to Smith, his vision was to get everything needed for service inside the building: "I didn't care what they did with the outside." Holland did not directly oppose Smith, but he unsuccessfully lobbied many groups to keep the

The Men's Gymnasium, Field House, and Rogers Field (left to right) during Holland's administration, 1939. *Ivan Shirrod Images Collection, pc117_390. WSU MASC.*

original design. In the end, the Holland Library had nine foot ceilings and the capacity to hold all of the library's collections after Smith and his colleagues completed a massive discard program of library materials stored in basements and attics across campus. William Stimson generously described Holland Library as a "building of clean, straight lines, trim and efficient, like a book lying on its side."

Holland died on Memorial Day, 1950, in a military hospital in Massachusetts. Holland was on his way to Vienna, Austria, on a higher education mission in the Army's program to remove Nazism from the European education system. The military doctors pronounced the cause of death as extreme exhaustion following two heart attacks earlier that year. Holland's sister, Edith Gifford, was by his bedside and reported Holland's last words, a question that reflected Holland's true Cougar spirit.

Image of Holland's plans for the new library, which he envisioned as a cathedral to learning with ceilings higher than the reading room of the University of Washington's grand Suzzallo Library. Holland's successors changed the plans. Washington State Alumni Powwow, *April 1944.*

Holland's funeral took place in the lobby of Holland Library where some 500 attended. Holland's colleagues recalled that he remembered the names and faces of people with whom had had even the slightest of contact. Ivy Lewellen, administrative assistant to Holland for twenty-seven years, said at Holland's memorial that "he was thoroughly honorable in all of his dealings." In addition to having the longest tenure of any WSU president, he was also one of its most dedicated administrators. His passion for collecting created the core of the campus's fine art, rare book, and manuscript collections. Holland steered WSC though challenging times and left it a larger, more vibrant institution. Much of the historic campus architecture hails from Holland's administration, as does the foundation of many of the academic programs. One of Holland's final legacies came to WSC fourteen years after his death—his estate gift of $410,000 (or more than three million when adjusted for inflation).

Research Notes

President Holland's tenure is the best documented of any of WSU's presidents. He wrote letters, thousands and thousands of them. Holland's papers held in Manuscripts, Archives, and Special Collections (MASC) comprise 325 boxes arranged in alphabetical order by year.

The official minutes of the WSU Board of Regents starting in 1891 are available online as are the *Evergreen* student newspaper and the *Chinook* yearbooks.

The papers of Henry Suzzallo, held in the University of Washington Libraries, include his correspondence with Holland—both their friendly exchanges and increasingly testy exchanges over curriculum and other issues.

Two books published by the Washington State University press in 1990 to celebrate the University centenary, William Stimson's *Going to Washington State: A Century of Student Life* and George Frykman's *Creating the Peoples University: Washington State University 1890 to 1990*, contain excellent chapters on Holland's administration. The only book length biography of a WSU president is William Landeen's *E. O. Holland and the State College of Washington 1916–1944*. Published in 1958, this volume is a fine administrative overview and a measured analysis of Holland's strengths and limitations.

A series of oral histories conducted as part of WSU's centennial and later expanded through Golden Grad class gifts and available in MASC provide a more critical view of Holland.

Wilson M. Compton

1945–1951

BY LARRY CLARK

As World War II drew toward its conclusion in 1944, WSC President Ernest Holland decided to step down. He had shepherded the college through World War I, the Great Depression, and much of the second world war, and he desired to hand off the baton and join the faculty ranks.

Campus had grown quieter that year. Fewer Air Force and Army cadets marched across the Pullman hills to training as they had over the first few years of the war. Many of the remaining WSC students were women, a record 1,348 of them, including some who had even moved into traditionally male Stimson and Waller Halls. WSC had a female student body president for the first time. Strains of tunes from the Andrews Sisters and Spokane native Bing Crosby, along with reports from WSC alumnus Edward R. Murrow, drifted around the sparsely populated campus, the soundtrack to an increasing anticipation of both the return of the soldiers and the arrival of the first new president at the college in almost 30 years.

When the search for a new leader in Pullman began, professors and students were eager to help with the selection of the president, perhaps someone already at the college. The Board of Regents interviewed

Wilson Compton, 1948.
WSU News Subject Files,
ua333b80f20. WSU MASC.

presidents of other colleges and universities around the country and after several months their eyes focused on a candidate on the other side of the continent.

The regents trekked to the other Washington and returned from the nation's capital with a most surprising choice: forest industry executive and lobbyist Wilson M. Compton.

The 54-year-old man with deep-set eyes, silver hair, and a dignified manner became not just a new president, but a new kind of leader at the small college on the Palouse. When he took the wheel in 1945, Compton moved to a campus on the verge of rapid change. A massive surge of students flooded WSC—GIs coming back from the battlefields, many of them married, with a strong independent streak after facing the horrors of war. This attitude didn't always mesh with the traditional college rules and culture, and the GI generation of Cougars tested the limits of WSC's housing, classrooms, and other facilities. They brought new demands regarding the role of the college in their lives and expanded their own leadership as students who shared in the college's operation.

Compton handled the influx with ingenuity and aplomb, endearing him to many of the students even in times of crisis and overcrowding. He and his wife Helen hosted students at their home, and he was often seen playing guitar and singing with them. Compton spoke of his vision for WSC students to gain skills for Washington industries like aerospace that flourished after the global conflict, while keeping a strong liberal arts tradition to graduate well-rounded men and women who would also be informed citizens. He also established student advising and counseling centers with less focus on the traditional, restrictive role of the dean of students.

At the same time, Compton forged WSC into a more professional and modern institution for faculty, with the first faculty manual, standardized reviews for instructors, and a committee for soliciting faculty opinions on curriculum and other matters—a precursor to the Faculty Senate.

However, Compton's desire to modernize led to conflict with some regents, faculty, and others who questioned his ambitious plans. This opposition, along with legislative budget shortfalls, eventually led to Compton's departure from the college. His years at Washington State remain a time of key transition, and much of what Compton started was integral to the college's transformation into a major research university.

WILSON MARTINDALE COMPTON WAS BORN ON OCTOBER 15, 1890, and raised in Wooster, Ohio, the second child in an academic family. His father Elias Compton was a Presbyterian minister and the first dean of philosophy at the College of Wooster. Wilson had two brothers—Karl and Arthur—and a sister Mary Elesia, all raised by their father and mother Otelia in a home that valued and required educational excellence.

The academic emphasis in the family led to their mother's selection by the Mother's Day Foundation as "the American mother" in 1939. Otelia's alma mater at Western College for Women in Oxford, Ohio, had even presented her a degree for "achievement as a mother."

The Compton family in formal dress. Standing in the back row are sons (left to right) Karl, Arthur, and Wilson. Seated in front of them (left to right) are Otelia and Elias. Their daughter, Mary, sits below them, to the front.
Courtesy College of Wooster Special Collections.

Wilson was pegged as a thinker from a young age. His mother encouraged it, indulging him for being late for dinner because he had been lost in his thoughts. "His thoughts are more important than eating," she would say.

All four Compton children graduated from the College of Wooster, and went on to Princeton University for graduate education. The three brothers were the first trio of siblings to earn doctoral degrees from that institution. Later the Comptons were the first three brothers to sit simultaneously at the helm of American colleges.

Karl T. Compton became a professor of physics and chairman of that department at Princeton, and later president of the Massachusetts Institute of Technology.

Younger brother Arthur H. Compton, also a physicist, researched the particle nature of electromagnetic rays, which earned him the Nobel Prize in Physics in 1927. As World War II engulfed the United States, he joined

The three Compton
brothers, left to right: Karl,
Arthur, and Wilson, 1945.
*Historic WSU Photographs
Collection, pc004b35a_
comptonguitarwbrothers.
WSU MASC.*

the Manhattan Project and was instrumental as head of the University of
Chicago laboratory responsible for designing nuclear reactors to produce
atomic bombs. He oversaw the work of Enrico Fermi in enriching urani-
um into plutonium, and the design of the graphite reactor in Oak Ridge,
Tennessee. After the war, he became chancellor of Washington University
in St. Louis around the time Wilson Compton became WSC president.

"The Compton Brothers were among the most illustrious alumni
of the Princeton Graduate School. . . . The trustees named one of the
two quadrangles which were added to the original Graduate College in
1963 the Compton Quadrangle in their honor," wrote Alexander Leitch
in *The Princeton Companion* in 1978.

Their sister Mary married a missionary, C. Herbert Rice, who headed
Forman Christian College in Lahore, India (later Pakistan).

Wilson earned renown not just for academic acumen but as a
four-sport athlete; in a single year he won letters in football, baseball,

basketball, and tennis at the College of Wooster. He earned his doctorate in economics from Princeton in 1915 and later his law degree from
Hamilton College. While studying there, he married Helen Mar Har-
rington of Bowling Green, Ohio, an energetic fellow Wooster graduate.
He taught at Dartmouth College for a little over a year.

Despite his educational pedigree, Wilson Compton did not plunge
full-time into academia after Dartmouth. Instead he wrote several
well-received articles on the difficulties of the forestry industry. That
launched 25 successful years in the forest products industry, after the
National Lumber Manufacturers Association (NLMA) asked him to
serve as the association's first secretary-manager.

"Compton was one of the most prominent of all trade association
leaders throughout the 1920s and 1930s," according to the Forest History Society. Compton turned the NLMA into a profitable, prominent
organization that came to wield great power within the lumber industry.

He helped resolve demobilization problems after the First World
War, worked to lessen competitive rivalries in the lumber industry, and
worked with government agencies, such as the U.S. Forest Service, to
produce cooperative programs. Compton built the NMLA public relations and trade promotion programs, and formed American Forest Products Industries and the Timber Engineering Company, which synced
well with the development of groundbreaking wood materials research
that began at WSC in 1949.

During the long tenure with the NMLA, the Comptons had settled
in rural Virginia outside of Washington on 1300-acre Seneca Farms,
which they stocked with Black Angus cattle, Hampshire sheep, and Du-
roc hogs. They also raised and experimented with hybrid corn adapted
for their region.

A new challenge now awaited the Comptons, though. Wilson's agricultural interests, success with the lumber industry, and deep connections in Washington, DC, drew the attention of a group from the West
seeking a president for their college, one who could move the institution
forward as the nation adjusted to a new era following World War II.

WHILE COMPTON MAY HAVE SEEMED A SURPRISE CHOICE for a small land-grant college in the Far West, the regents recognized he had the national profile and the business acumen they would need to modernize the institution as service members returned and industry pivoted to peace-time. Compton had deep connections in the federal government, particularly the U.S. Department of Agriculture, which could benefit the college.

It also helped to have a famous name. Weeks before his inauguration in 1945 as president of Washington State, *Life* magazine featured all three Compton brothers in a photo and highlighted their contributions to physics, the war effort, and higher education.

The Board of Regents announced Compton's selection on August 21, 1944, and Compton accepted the position two months later in October.

Many Washington newspaper editorials also applauded the selection and declared Compton a practical man who could lead the college in the right direction for the state. The *Spokesman-Review* said Compton would contribute greatly "to the scientific growth and expansion of the Pullman institution."

But the enthusiasm for the new president was not universal. Gubernatorial candidate and eventual governor Monrad Wallgren blasted Compton for his lack of connections to the state and agriculture. Wallgren questioned whether Compton could serve agriculture when the vast portion of his experience was with "lumber barons." After Wallgren was elected, he and Compton had a relatively stable relationship, but the governor began appointing new regents, some of whom had little appreciation for Compton's plans and goals.

On the Washington State College campus the excitement was palpable, though.

It was a warm and hazy fall in 1944 when Compton made his first official visit to Pullman. On October 17, he pulled in a huge crowd with just a few hours' notice; more than 2,100 faculty, students, and staff packed Bryan Hall beyond capacity to hear the new president.

Harry E. Goldsworthy, president of the Board of Regents, introduced Compton to the gathered collegians with great praise: "Had there ever been a doubt as to the standing of the State College, certainly it was dispelled for the regents this summer when for nearly six months we have been in contact with nearly all the colleges and universities of the country in our painstaking search for that rare man who could take up where President Holland leaves off. Today, we have such a man."

Compton addressed the audience as "a fellow freshman of WSC," and heaped kudos on the Holland administration's work to expand academics and the physical campus. He made it clear he would consult with the faculty and Holland before considering any changes.

A couple of days later, Compton talked to 150 Pullman Kiwanis members and their guests and urged "continuation of close contact between hill and town." He repeated that nothing would be changed merely for the sake of change, but made it clear he was not afraid of innovations.

He told of his life as a youth in a small town "about the size of Pullman." Compton, heralding back to his early sports career, said he wanted an "early resumption of intercollegiate athletics on a pre-war basis" with the hope that students would have fun, so long as scholastic standards were not compromised.

Compton also met with student leaders over dinner in the Commons to talk about his ideas for the college, with the *Evergreen* reporting, "Dr. Compton with his sense of humor, won the hearts of the representatives during the evening."

Compton's vision for WSC quickly became clear to all the college faculty, staff, students, and leadership. During his inaugural speech on December 11, 1945, he said:

> The State College of Washington aims to contribute to the life of the Pacific Northwest in an unending stream of educated young men and women, well-trained, professionally competent, conscious of civic duty, individually capable of constructive leadership in American life.

It aims to encourage, inspire, and implement the advancement of agriculture, industry, and commerce. It aims to extend more broadly to all the people of the state its facilities for aiding in the economic and cultural development of the Northwest, for the advancement of interest in public health and public welfare.

It didn't take long before Compton's "unending stream" of students would become a tidal wave.

EVERYONE FORESAW THE POST-WAR SURGE IN COLLEGE students even before Compton's arrival at WSC. They just didn't realize how the massive numbers would transform the college. As World War II ended in 1945, the Servicemen's Readjustment Act of 1944—commonly known as the GI Bill of Rights—offered opportunity for the scores of soldiers returning to the United States with a guarantee of free tuition and weekly stipends for living expenses. In the peak year of 1947, veterans accounted for 49 percent of college admissions nationwide.

The effect on Washington State, as at many colleges and universities, was profound. Soon after Compton started his presidency at the beginning of 1945, he set a policy that no academically qualified veteran would be denied admission. Subsequently, enrollment skyrocketed from 2,700 to 7,000. The 1947 *Chinook* yearbook opened with a series of student-filled photos of the campus, with the caption "Crowded, Isn't It?"

Many of the GIs "arrived on campus wearing uniform remnants—a warm sailor's peacoat, army tan pants, or unpolished government-issue boots," wrote William L. Stimson in *Going to Washington State: A Century of Student Life*. They didn't fit the old mold of traditional college students, either. The new student-veterans were more mature, intent on receiving an education, often married, and unwilling to merely accept the status quo.

The old codes of conduct and the hierarchical systems among students, such as forcing freshmen to wear beanies, did not suit the young men who had seen the horrors of war.

Compton by the fireplace in
the president's house in 1945.
WSU News Subject Files,
ua333b80f20n04064b.
WSU MASC.

The overwhelming number of independent GIs changed the dynamic in student government as well. The 1947 student president Dick
Downing, for example, was a married veteran with two children. The
independents promoted practical interests: better food, more housing,
less mud around the dorms. They also took a firm position on issues
like the need for a permanent student union building.

The TUB, a converted gymnasium, was large enough for dances and
dinners, and had a smaller hangout space in its basement called "The
Drain." While the students adapted the space with a jukebox playing
Frank Sinatra and Perry Como, Saturday dances, coffee, and burgers,
the TUB just wasn't big enough to meet the needs of everyone.

The temporary student union exemplified the physical limitations of
the college, and Compton immediately set to work in 1945 to relieve the

coming pressures on housing, classrooms, and other facilities resulting from the massive increase in students.

During his tenure, eight major buildings were completed between 1946 and 1951. The completion of Todd Hall in 1949 gave the college an urgently needed instructional building. It was the first completely air-conditioned and was the largest classroom building on campus.

Other buildings constructed during Compton's presidency that remain on campus include the L. J. Smith Agricultural Engineering Building, built in 1947, and the Washington State Institute of Technology Building and the Mining Experiment Station (later Dana Hall), built in 1948.

A signature building of the Compton era was almost delayed. The new library, to be named after Ernest Holland, was planned but fell to a lower priority in Compton's wish list of building projects to the state legislature.

Compton saw other projects, such as housing and classrooms, as more pressing needs for the campus. However, former president Holland leveraged his influence with Governor Mon Wallgren to push the library project, and soon it appeared at the top of the governor's list.

The Holland Library was completed in the summer of 1950 as a leading example of modular architecture. It provided space for a million volumes and 2,200 college students, with walls designed to be modified according to the needs of library users. Its straight, utilitarian lines certainly didn't meet Holland's desire to match the University of Washington's Suzzallo Library, but it garnered praise for its solid pragmatism.

The new permanent and renovated structures still failed to handle the sheer numbers of students. Quonset huts and cramped classrooms barely contained the GI students for academics. Aging buildings, limited lab space, and outmoded lighting and facilities were just a few of the complaints from faculty members who saw their classrooms packed with students.

The housing situation was dire as well. When the bulk of the GIs came to campus in 1947, housing for students was an enormous problem. To cope with the shortage, Compton negotiated for war surplus housing to be dismantled at either no cost or practically nothing and reconstructed in Pullman. The college even became landlord for a number of houses on nearby Military Hill. Subsequently, student housing was increased to 223 family units and more than 3,000 dormitory units.

Despite the college's best efforts, housing wasn't the most pleasant experience. On campus, the wood sections from the surplus housing became four big GI dorms: North House (on the site of the future French Administration building), South House (across Farm Way, today's Grimes Way, from North House), East House, and West House (below the current Fine Arts Building). The long, two-story buildings looked and felt like barracks to the veterans, with thin bunks, poor heating, and squeaky floors.

Built for 385 residents, the structures were bursting with nearly 500 students at one point. The landscape around the new dorms conjured memories of slogging through battlefields; the area became known as "Mud Hollow," as the mushy farmland around the buildings splattered the shoes and pants of students making their way up the hill to class.

Still, Compton felt WSC's record in handling the housing of veteran students was done with the best of intentions. "We had to improvise a great deal to handle the GIs," he said. "But we are proud to say that no qualified veteran who was interested, earnest, and determined enough actually to come to WSC in person to enroll, was turned away from the State College of Washington. Some, it is true, could not find housing, so could not stay. But most did."

Compton also oversaw the construction of a new women's dormitory, the Regents Hill Complex, to house almost 400 women, although it didn't open until 1952 following Compton's departure from the college.

The lack of housing also struck the staff. In order to build up the faculty to handle the increase in enrollment, more housing was needed in Pullman. The college provided 200 family units in addition to other dormitory units for faculty and staff. The Comptons themselves pitched in, as Compton wrote in 1946. "In my own home during the past year, we have had twenty-seven students and faculty members and their families, including my own household."

THE PRESIDENT'S HOME AT LEAST HAD UNDERGONE SOME beautification to host those guests. A major driver of many physical changes on campus came not only from Wilson, but also from wife Helen Compton's endless energy and enthusiasm. She and Mary Warner, her housekeeper and general assistant, began improving the president's house by removing antiquated stone gateways, planting flowers and shrubbery, and redecorating the interior.

It didn't stop with her own residence. She took a very direct role in renovating old houses around town for the increased number of faculty members and wasn't afraid of hard work. She and Warner were sometimes seen picking up shingles torn from a roof being resurfaced or wielding a paint brush.

Helen Compton was known for her sharp eye for landscaping. She procured thousands of tulip and daffodil bulbs for planting on the campus—at no cost. Even the new construction received her touch; Todd Hall walls were painted pastel colors at her request, to brighten the classrooms.

Even as she took a lead in campus construction, Compton kept up a busy schedule of entertaining students, staff, and visitors. The president's house became known as the "Compton's Hotel," because there always seemed to be house guests.

In 1948, the Comptons bought a shuttered resort on Priest Lake in northern Idaho, and offered a number of lots for faculty and staff members to purchase. Helen Compton and Warner applied their skills to rejuvenating Beaver Creek, as it was renamed. The rustic academic retreat gave faculty and their families a place of incredible solitude. They needed to be ferried there by boat, which were surplus Navy ship-to-shore launches that Helen Compton had secured. Days were spent huckleberry picking with the Comptons, swimming, and working to clean up and renovate the cabins.

The always-busy Mrs. Compton took on another off-campus project used by WSC, a ski lodge near Emida, Idaho, about an hour from Pullman.

Her efforts weren't universally appreciated. Some students chafed at her sudden appearances and "advice" on how to beautify or reorganize their apartments and homes.

"Helen Compton served as an unofficial inspector general, constantly searching the campus for problems that needed to be fixed," wrote Stimson in *Going to Washington State*. No detail was too small. She ordered old Ferry Hall urinals replaced, buildings painted, and was known to drop in unexpectedly on married students. A 1949 cartoon in the WSC student humor magazine *Fo Paws* even showed Helen Compton telling a bird how to build a nest.

The complaints sometimes climbed all the way to the Board of Regents, where members antagonistic to Compton railed against his wife's real estate dealing and busybody attitude toward students and faculty.

EVEN WITH HELEN COMPTON'S INCESSANT INVOLVE-ment in students' lives, the Comptons received plenty of accolades from the student body. Wilson Compton, despite his dignified demeanor, was, perhaps surprisingly, seen as caring and conscientious of student needs.

Veteran students in particular meant a lot to the Comptons. Their two sons and a son-in-law had served during the war, and Compton said their service was a key reason for his move into higher education.

Compton often said he wished he could spend more time with students. To bridge the gap, he and his wife frequently opened the doors of their home. They initiated the annual "Pig Dinner" at their home for the presidents of college living groups during the Christmas season. Photos show Compton playing guitar and singing with groups of students on his lawn.

One student acquainted with Compton said: "Dr. Compton is a wonderful, fatherly man. Both he and Mrs. Compton are the kind of people you'd like to know better. They're just good, natural folks."

Compton also had a sly sense of humor and was willing to go along with a good joke. "You can't describe that chuckle, or the grin that

Walla Walla radio station owner Herb Studebaker receives a
plaque from Compton as Helen Compton watches. *Historic WSU
Photographs Collection, pc004b35a_compton. WSU MASC.*

sometimes turns so boyish you have the feeling you knew him as a
particularly mischievous twelve-year-old," a friend said in 1951. "Much
of the point of his humor is in his inflection and his facial expression."

That same friend added, "Under that dignity and incomparable
poise, he's a thoroughly human individual—and he has his faults. I
think the most basic one I've seen is an extreme slowness to recognize
the pettiness in persons less big than himself."

As Compton promised in his inaugural address, he began the realignment of the college to match the needs of industries in the state.
He saw those main players as agriculture and aerospace. To that end,

Compton established the "twin institutes," the Institute of Agricultural Sciences and the Institute of Technology. The latter included the College of Engineering, School of Mines, Engineering Experiment Station, Mining Experiment Station, State Electrometallurgical Laboratories, and the Divisions of Industrial Research and Industrial Services. The other included the College of Agriculture, Agricultural Extension Service, and Agricultural Experiment Stations.

To keep WSC's work in these areas closely tied to the state's agriculture and industry, Compton set up an advisory board for each institute made up of leaders active in those fields. Training students and investing in research would improve the economy, according to Compton.

However, that didn't preclude a more general education for students. Integrated courses in humanities, biological and physical sciences, and the social sciences all became part of the curriculum at Compton's and the faculty's urging.

"It is as important that trained men be educated as that educated men be trained," Compton declared about a broad program for WSC students.

He also pushed a reorganization of the College of Sciences and Arts into four divisions: humanities, biological sciences, social sciences, and physical sciences. While it seemed fairly innocuous, it gave authority to chairs of those divisions to integrate the technical and liberal arts education.

That did not sit well with the deans and heads of professional programs. The dean of the School of Pharmacy objected angrily to the idea of outside faculty advising his students. In early 1950, a group of scientists protested about the "awkward" arrangement that could diminish their programs.

Vice President E. H. Hopkins, appointed by Compton to handle the reorganization of the college, couldn't quell the rebellion. Eventually the professional program leaders garnered support from outside organizations, and the Board of Regents took authority away from the division chairs after hearing complaints from both inside and outside of WSC.

Despite the internal squabbles, Compton extended instruction more broadly to all people of the state through the "Little WSCs," an expansion of the Community College Service program. Beginning a year after Compton took over, three off-campus educational centers were established by the college, with most of the staff coming from resident faculty in Pullman. In 1947, WSC centers were set up in Pasco and Spokane, and in 1949 another was established in Yakima. The Pasco Center closed in 1949 and the Yakima Center closed in 1951.

Harkening to the land-grant vision of the college, WSC increased "short course" educational opportunities for all Washingtonians. These classes, lasting from one day to a week, brought together people in a given field—agriculture, industry, banking, and many others—to discuss their problems with WSC experts.

Compton had even proposed a Spokane campus for the college, first at Baxter Hospital, which was soundly rejected by the WSC faculty. Later, the site of Fort George Wright in Spokane offered another option. That deal fell through, too, as a group from Spokane secured the fort from the Army as a reserve depot, just as Compton was lobbying in Washington, DC, for what would have been Washington State's first branch campus.

THE EDUCATIONAL REALIGNMENT AND EXPANSION OF the college, controversial though it may have been, seemed relatively small compared to the long-lasting effects that Compton began in changing the very governance of the institution.

He had been appointed as president, in part, to modernize the college. On Compton's second day in office, he received authority to establish a committee of faculty to review the entire State College. The "Committee of Forty," led by young economics associate professor John Guthrie, dove in immediately and delivered a number of recommendations in short order.

They said faculty, staff, and students should have the right to organize without administrative interference. The committee also said its own role should continue indefinitely to advise the administration and represent all faculty, a precursor to the Faculty Senate.

"For the first time the faculty was given a voice in the running of the school, and it was a critical step in the direction of the college becoming a true university," WSU historian George Frykman said in a 1990 interview.

The regents agreed "in principle" with the Committee of Forty's and Compton's recommendation to require codified regulations for faculty and staff, instead of the often-biased past treatment on such matters as salaries, research, teaching loads, and off-campus work. What eventually became the faculty manual also cemented modern ideas like tenure for professors.

The tenure concept for faculty members had become more prominent after standards were established in 1940 by the American Association of University Professors. It really took off in 1945 with the faculty shortages spurred by the GI bulge. Compton wanted the tenure carrot, along with published peer review and other standards, to bring in more young, talented faculty. In the interests of academic freedom and retaining high-quality professors, the regents approved the tenure proposal in 1949.

Not all of the regents or faculty members were fully supportive of some of the changes. In particular, the idea of peer review for faculty, rather than a more top-down assessment—which they could control—rubbed some regents the wrong way.

In addition to the faculty changes, Compton increased student autonomy by moving archaic administrative positions like the dean of women into a student counseling service, as well as pushing for more student self-governance.

The new counseling and activities programs gave students more opportunity to obtain help for themselves. Although students truly appreciated the shift, many faculty members and regents began to grouse about the expense of the student advising programs.

The GI students and others, though, wanted less strict "parental" control and more independence. They also weren't going to wait for WSC administrators or faculty to push important needs like better housing and a student union.

In 1949 a student delegation lobbied the legislature in Olympia for money to build a new, larger student union. For the first time, students from Pullman involved themselves in the political efforts surrounding financial support of the college.

"We had two or three carloads of kids who went to Olympia," said 1950 graduate Bill Fitch, a student leader at the time. "In those days, we had an activist, 'get it done' attitude."

The state leaders rewarded them with the Compton Union Building, the CUB, which, even today, remains the heart of the Pullman campus.

The same "get it done" attitude helped Compton and the campus community overcome disaster in 1948. As part of the housing solution, a huge trailer court known as "Trailerville" along the banks of Paradise Creek below campus became home to 304 married students.

On January 7, 1948, the creek swelled and threatened to swamp Trailerville with a surge three feet higher than the trailer court's ground level. Around 500 students and Pullman residents built a dike of 20,000 sandbags filled with split peas and sand, which diverted the water.

"Unfortunately, that day's record as 'worst ever flood' was short lived, and a month and a half later, on February 21, the creek's waters rose up and threatened the camp again, this time a full foot deeper than January's flood," wrote WSU archivist Mark O'English. The students and townspeople built an even larger dike, and once again saved the trailer court.

Four days later, the waters of Paradise Creek rose one more time, higher than the previous two floods, overwhelming the sandbag dam, swamping the trailers, and trapping many of the sleeping residents, who were rescued by a "human chain" of volunteers. Compton opened a cafeteria to flood victims and offered his house as a staging center for displaced students. Within 12 hours, all had found places to stay.

COMPTON'S VISIONARY IDEAS WEREN'T LIMITED TO THE college or even the state. As early as 1945, he foresaw not only the industrial transformation of Washington in areas like aerospace and modernized agriculture, but also the importance of trade with Asia and other trans-Pacific partners.

He did more than talk about the importance of the college to globalism and trade. In 1946, General Douglas MacArthur invited Compton to Japan to serve on an educational mission. His activities in the international field were expanded when he served as an alternate delegate for the United States to the United Nations General Assembly in 1949.

Under Compton, the number of international students at WSC also rose significantly, leading to development of English classes for those students from countries with other languages.

The president also saw the need for the American students to understand the new global environment. In a January 1951 speech, Compton laid out again his belief in the value of the college in advancing the nation.

"Public education is said to be at the heart of free society. Public education is certainly at the heart of the magnificent system of production which has enabled our nation with less than 7 percent of the world's population to produce nearly 50 percent of the world's goods. We cannot compete with the populous nations of the world in terms of manpower, but we can compete in terms of horsepower," he said.

Despite Compton's high-minded goals, his contentious relationship with some of the regents came to a head in early 1951, as state support for the college waned and enrollment dipped as GIs graduated.

Compton recommended a number of staff and program cuts to deal with the budget crunch, which provided an opportunity for some of the regents to rein him in. His reforms in faculty governance and realignment of departments angered some faculty members and deans.

Compton's main detractor, regent and prominent Episcopal minister Charles McAllister, led the charge against the president. He had written a book about college governance himself and disagreed with Compton's ambitious moves.

Compton at the groundbreaking ceremony for the future Compton
Union Building, May 29, 1949. He is joined by student leaders and
the Board of Regents, including Charles E. McAllister, just to
the left of Compton at center. McAllister would lead the drive to
fire the president in the coming months. *MASC Negatives Files,
pc149b5n88-194. WSU MASC.*

The board voted to cut funding for student advising and counseling
and to eliminate the position of vice president, effectively firing Compton's trusted lieutenant E. H. Hopkins. Compton opposed these moves.

At the end of April 1951, McAllister gathered enough support to force
Compton's resignation. Compton had tendered a letter of resignation as
a courtesy when he accepted the position in 1944. McAllister was happy
to accept it after his squabbles with the president.

THE REACTION TO COMPTON'S FIRING WAS SWIFT AND widespread.

When word came to the students, Compton was out of town, so student leaders led by student body president Dave Nordquist met him at the Spokane airport. They arrived on campus to a gathering reminiscent of Compton's greeting back in 1944: several hundred students waited on Rogers Field to see him.

"I was disappointed when Wilson Compton left," said Bill Fitch. "He put Washington State on the map at a pivotal, developmental point."

The students realized Compton had faced controversy. When addressing the students, though, he made sure that the *fait accompli* of his firing didn't cause any unrest.

A few days later, the Faculty Executive Committee issued a statement that they were "profoundly shocked by the unexpected resignation of its president . . . and earnestly regrets that the College is to lose his strong and constructive leadership." They also expressed a desire to continue many of Compton's policies.

From across the state, Raymond B. Allen, the president of the University of Washington, wrote a letter of appreciation for Compton that showed his strong working relationship with the WSC president and summed up much of what Compton had accomplished:

> The face of the Washington State College campus has been changed even in a period when much of Dr. Compton's time necessarily was occupied by matters of administration and finance. But all of us who know him well realize that his greatest satisfactions come from his associations with students and with his faculty. . . . Under his leadership, the State College had set for itself a goal of performance which one day will place the College in a position of international leadership.
>
> Today, with the nation and the world in crisis, it is more important than ever that the state and its tax paying citizens realize the deep significance . . . of the contributions made by these two institutions, and all higher education, to national security and national welfare.

There can be no future without sound education, no security that is
not rooted in the intellectual vigor and productivity of our colleges
and universities. It was to this truth that Dr. Compton dedicated his
work as president.

Compton's dismissal rippled across the nation as well. *Life* magazine
didn't mince words with the headline published in June 1951: "Picture
of a Good Man Who is Getting the Ax."

"Energetic, popular Wilson Compton had if anything been too ambitious for W.S.C.," they wrote. "In his six years as president he had produced new buildings, seen enrollment climb from 1,500 to 6,000 and had
envisioned the college as a top-notch educational center in the Northwest.

"Two weeks ago the regents met with faculty and student representatives, issued a statement 'differences of opinion' on the 'relative
importance of various phases' of the college. Said Compton, 'I assented
[to the statement], but I'm still mystified.'"

Life also printed a few letters in July in response to the article. One,
from former WSC Regent Walter Robinson, commended the magazine
for highlighting what he thought was an ill-considered decision. Another
missive from previous alumni director Oscar Jones, though, stated that
a large number of students and faculty disliked Compton's policies,
and that a bunch of new buildings did not justify the magazine's high
praise for Compton.

The most thoughtful letter came from George Goudy, who became
student body president in 1952, and Keith Jackson of future sports broad-
casting fame, freshman class president. They claimed Compton's greatest
achievement was not new buildings "but the personal fatherly touch he
has maintained with the students."

Compton himself responded with a more forthright statement on
his firing. In the letter, quoted in the *Evergreen*, he wrote "The Board
of Regents during the past two years has been largely reconstituted by
six appointments to a board of seven members. The Board as now con-
stituted has favored certain policies for the College and concerning its
presidency with which I have not been in entire sympathy. I have felt
that as its president I could be helpful to the State College, to its students

Presidents Raymond Allen of University of Washington (left) and
Wilson Compton of Washington State, shown in 1950, shared
a strong working relationship. *WSU Publications and Printing
Photographs, pc001b01n00650. WSU MASC.*

and faculty, and to the state's growing agriculture and industry only if I
had the confidence and support of the Board of Regents, as I have had
of the students, faculty, and staff."

That support from students and WSC employees helped keep some
of Compton's more controversial policies in place even after his departure. On May 25, 1951, almost a month after the regents accepted
Compton's resignation, they issued a joint statement with student body
president Bill Green, Dean of the Faculty S. Town Stephenson, and

chair of the Faculty Executive Committee John Guthrie affirming and cementing some of Compton's top achievements. They agreed to adhere to the faculty manual, especially in procedures such as personnel policy (including appointments, promotions, salaries, tenure, pensions, and terminations of service).

The group also gave students, alumni, and faculty the opportunity to address the Board of Regents directly, take part in the selection of the college's president, and continue the revised structure of student advising.

THE COMPTONS RETURNED TO SENECA FARMS, THEIR home in Virginia. Compton did not hold any resentment toward the college. He returned to Pullman for homecoming in the fall of 1952 for the dedication of the CUB, the student union building named after him.

Compton returned to public service shortly after his presidency. Between 1952 and 1953, he was director of the International Information Administration, the forerunner of the United States Information Agency, within the Department of State.

He left this job just two years later due to conflicting differences with Senator Joseph McCarthy. Compton served as director of the Council for Financial Aid to Education until his retirement in 1959.

The Comptons retired to Wooster, Ohio. Wilson Compton died on March 7, 1967, at age 76.

COMPTON'S SHORT SIX YEARS AT WASHINGTON STATE College witnessed a transformation unlike anything in the history of the institution, with a more than 300 percent increase in enrollment, 200 percent growth in housing facilities for students and staff, and 100 percent increase in other construction on campus. He oversaw over $14 million dollars in capital improvements, with another $5 million in construction underway when he left. A huge new library and classroom building, labs stocked with war surplus equipment to train students and aid research, and a permanent student union building all had Compton's stamp on them.

Beyond Pullman, the college saw an expansion in prestige and reputation during Wilson Compton's presidency. His broad vision led to the transformation into a major public university less than a decade after he left.

Compton had laid out that vision for Washington State years before. In his prescient January 1946 inauguration speech, Compton said that, by 1960, "I see a great center of industrial and agricultural technologies with modern laboratories, housing great scientists; a library which has it and can find it when you want it; a Student Union, the congenial campus meeting place of 10,000 young men and women . . . a place for married students . . . a busy airport, a few more Vince Hansons [a student athlete who excelled in baseball, basketball, and track], and a great rush for seats on the 50-yard line."

His most lasting contribution, though, is likely the shift toward faculty independence and professionalism. Compton standardized faculty evaluation, started a faculty manual with written employment regulations and rights, improved retirement and pension plans for faculty and staff, and established a faculty senate to take a role in governing the institution. Thanks to his leadership, these changes remain at the core of academic freedom and crucial to the continued success of Washington State.

Research Notes

This essay on Wilson Compton's life and six-year stint as Washington State College president draws on a mixture of newspapers, magazines, histories, and Compton's speeches. He did love giving a speech, apparently at great length.

Newspapers such as WSC's own *Evergreen*, the *Pullman Daily Herald*, and the *Spokesman-Review* provided anecdotes and a sense of the period, as did the WSC alumni publication, *The Powwow*, and the students' annual *Chinook* yearbook. *Life* magazine featured the Compton family more than once, which gave a national perspective on Wilson Compton.

Specialized histories from the forest industry group, Princeton University, and the College of Wooster helped paint a portrait of Wilson as a young (and middle-aged) man. Essays by WSU archivist Mark O'English and interviews with Washington State alumni of the Compton era filled in more of that picture.

Two fine histories of Washington State's history published in 1990—*Going to Washington State: A Century of Student Life* by William Stimson and *Creating the People's University: Washington State University 1890 to 1990* by George Frykman—provided detail and deeper understanding of the significant shifts at the college.

C. Clement French
1952–1966

BY SAM FLEISCHER

A. Bartlett Giamatti, former president of Yale University, said that leadership was a moral act. It was the assertion of a vision, not simply the exercise of a style. The tenure of Washington State University president Charles Clement French clearly reveals a moral visionary ahead of his time.

French's term as WSU's president saw tremendous growth in the size and stature of the institution. He was guided throughout his life by principles he extolled regularly at Washington State: the commitment to education as part of a duty to community and good will toward society. This vision of the sixth president of Washington State University was a perspective and focus he developed early in life, forged during his spiritual youth and subsequent high school years coinciding with World War I. He never wavered from this vision.

C. Clement French was born on October 24, 1901, in Philadelphia, in a new century defined by a rise in international warfare and the struggle for democracy around the globe. He graduated

C. Clement French, around age 35
(undated). *C. Clement French Papers,
cg310b5f24. WSU MASC.*

from Northwest High School, an all-boys school, in June 1918. At his
graduation ceremony the Salutary was titled, "American Ideals and
the War," while the Valedictory—"The High School Graduate in War
Time"—reinforced the reality that French and his classmates were entering a world of conflict, where duty was necessary.

French delivered the graduation address entitled "Food and the
War." In his speech, he voiced the belief and vision that those in supporting roles back home had an obligation to men in the war, and local
failure to support the front lines with enough corn and wheat carried
with it patriotic stain. Already, French had formed an ideal that those
with educational opportunities had a sacred duty to contribute to the
benefit of society, as a way to preserve democracy in America. French
would repeat this sentiment, a moral vision reinforced through years of
academic leadership, many times in his life.

He completed three degrees at the University of Pennsylvania by 1927,
culminating in his doctorate in physical chemistry. When French's thesis, "The Effect of Neutral Salts on Certain Catalytic Decompositions,"

was published in the *Journal of Physical Chemistry* a year later, his name appeared as "C. Clement French" for the first time, the professional identity that would stick forever. By then French also was married: Helen Augusta Black proved to be a perfect fit for him. She earned her A.B. from Ohio State University in 1924, and on Christmas Day, 1925, they tied the knot. For the rest of his life French would call Helen his equal partner, both privately and publicly. He often noted the WSU presidency was a two-person job, and Helen's presence at many public functions for the university demonstrated this. Leadership is not just about one person; it is about the organization and its stakeholders. French never forgot this simple truth and how it related to his vision of duty in public and private life.

French was deeply influenced by spirituality throughout his life. He descended from Quakers who came to the American colonies in the late seventeenth century and was raised in the teachings of the Society of Friends, which emphasized service to others. This upbringing also shaped his brother Paul, who was the executive director of the Cooperative for American Remittances Everywhere (CARE) from 1946 to 1955. This combination of nurturing and world awareness formed French's moral vision. A lifetime of involvement in faith-oriented groups and organizations reinforced his philosophy. Immanuel Kant believed nothing makes a person moral; individuals must do that on their own. The individual contributes to the whole, whereas actions are guided by the universal moral law established collectively. This in many ways reflects the core of French's moral vision in leadership.

In his final commencement address at WSU in May 1966, he stated,

> I hope as you go out this afternoon, graduated, you will remember that you do have an obligation to the institution and to the society that made this possible for you. Many of you, and certainly I, in another society, would not have had the opportunity that you and I have had. Consequently, it behooves each of us to remember that along with what has been possible for us there is the responsibility for seeing this continues, improved and bettered, for those who follow.

Helen and C. Clement
French at faculty reception on
WSC campus, April 25, 1952.
*C. Clement French Papers,
cg310b5f23. WSU MASC.*

The moral vision which defined French's leadership at WSU was
grounded in the man at a very young age, and that sense of duty—
driven by what Kant called a good will—would remain with him for
life, to the tremendous benefit of all those he came in contact with over
the decades. French did not just arrive in Pullman magically ready to
lead: he had cut his teeth for a quarter of century in higher education,
developing as an administrator and growing as a leader, the result of his
lifelong sense of duty.

IN THE QUARTER CENTURY BETWEEN EARNING HIS DOC-
torate and his arrival in Pullman, French acquired experience in varying
higher education roles on the East Coast and in the South. He stayed at
Penn for three years in a postdoctoral teaching capacity before taking a
faculty position at Randolph-Macon Women's College in Lynchburg,

Virginia. From 1930 to 1949, he was head of the chemistry department and also dean of the college.

As dean, French passed on what he believed was the most important ideal to colleagues, peers, and students: education and its subsequent duty to society. French believed in the role of America's education system for democracy, and this reflected prominently in his work and relationships. In the October 1952 issue of *The Washington Newspaper*, he stated, "The American people have always believed that as the individual develops, society as a whole gains. We have held to the theory that not only in the development of superior vocational and professional competence, but in the development of the general liberal education of the members of the body politic, there is a gain to the whole group."

In 1949 French departed for Virginia Polytechnic Institute in Blacksburg to serve as vice president. While at VPI, French worked with a newly arrived university president, and by spring 1950 the administration was earning public praise for its efforts and progress. His leadership already making an impact, French's selfless approach to education was on display and getting him noticed nationally. This experience at a land-grant institution under a capable senior administrator, leading a proud academic institution of higher learning to new achievements, improved his understanding of campus culture.

Leaders seek to bring members of their organization into alignment with the culture and mission of the institution; individuals need to be empowered by leadership to understand their ambitions also are in line with the organization's goals. That ability makes leadership work effectively, and French learned this at VPI, merging his individual vision—which already focused on the greater good—with the needs of the campus. This blend worked very well at a land-grant institution, with its inherent mission to serve the community.

Success opened up opportunities for French, and by fall 1950 he had moved to College Station, Texas, to become dean at Texas Agricultural and Mechanical College (now Texas A&M). As with his experience at VPI, he arrived in conjunction with a new university president at a land-grant institution. Not surprisingly, his efforts again were noticed around the country. French had just turned 50 and was ready for his own presidency. In response to overtures from the campus in Pullman, Washington, the Frenches initially declined, as they had two college-aged children enrolled in higher education. Born in January 1930, Jane graduated from Southern Methodist University in December 1951 after transferring from VPI. Richard, born in December 1932, attended A&M for two years before following his parents to Pullman and eventually graduating from Washington State in 1954.

A wise leader chooses the right situation—and declines the wrong one. Leadership also starts with awareness. Without knowing the issues in an organization, leaders cannot be effective. Before French chose to take the presidency at Washington State, he had turned down various offers from other schools, including Louisiana State University, the University of Massachusetts at Amherst, and the University of North Carolina. With his experiences at VPI and A&M, he knew the job opening in Pullman offered the best fit for his educational vision. The Washington State hiring committee liked French, as he emerged from an original candidate pool of 323 to stand out in the selection process.

French had the capability of bringing individuals together in harmony and honesty, as demonstrated in the interview and selection process. By February 1952 he had accepted the position and was preparing to move to Pullman. He once said, "I was unafraid to make decisions, but that decision making to me became a matter of working with people and talking things over with them, but being unafraid to decide in the end the difficult things." Pullman represented an opportunity for growth and the chance for many in the state of Washington, and beyond, to benefit. French wasted no time, choosing an immediate transition to the presidency. Instead of waiting for the term to end, the Frenches arrived by April in order to start work right away.

French was ready for the challenge.

WASHINGTON STATE FACED DIFFICULT BUDGET CUTS when French began work on April 1, 1952. He did so with little fanfare. The humble beginnings of French's tenure were commended in a June 16, 1952, article in the *Daily Evergreen* as he minimized ceremony surrounding his arrival. The student newspaper noted, "Informality and the personal approach took over the campus as Dr. C. Clement French was officially installed in the presidency at commencement June 1— with none other than the new president disclaiming it as highlight of graduation exercises." Never one to attract attention to himself, "French quickly turned the emphasis back to the graduates, saying they were the center of the day." This was a leader focused on the organization and its needs, not needing to bathe himself in adoration. The *Daily Evergreen* eloquently concluded the WSC students were honored: "All of them are likely to remember, so long as their memory runs, that it was in a background of chimes and sunshine at the 56th commencement that he formally was given and accepted responsibility for leading the State College of Washington."

The budget cuts were based on the assumption that veterans on the G.I. Bill would be graduating, thus reducing enrollment. However, WSC was about to begin its most significant growth in history.

French's vision for WSC was exemplified in his requests for increases in state funding. When he respectfully implored the 1955 state legislature for a 17 percent increase in funding for WSC, French argued, "The function of the state college of Washington is to serve the people of the state—you and your sons and daughters—through its educational, research, and extension activities." He had understood for decades that education serves the people, the state, and the nation—and by the extension of democracy and its enlightened citizenry, the world. French appealed to the legislature's sense of personal obligation in order to get the funding Washington State needed in a brilliant display of moral leadership.

On campus, French quickly established an accessible leadership style as well. Dad's Day in fall 1952 featured a home football game against

Stanford University. Attached to every game program was a personal note from Helen and Clement: "We hope you enjoy the game, and may the better team win. Immediately following the game we will be 'at home' in the President's House. You are cordially invited to stop there for coffee or punch before starting your return drive." Opening his doors to everyone demonstrated French's ability to involve all stakeholders as well as his desire to be just another person on campus, working for the greater good of the organization. Another example of his accessibility came when French oversaw the opening of the Wilson Compton Union, noting publicly that, "With the opening of the Wilson Compton Union, the WSC community—students, faculty, and staff—has the opportunity for a new and rich experience in campus-centered activity. This building can become the 'living room' of the campus for all of us. It will provide a place for informal contact which will further advance the friendly relations so long existing among the various parts of WSC."

This was French's way of bringing the campus together in reaction to the controversy over the naming of the building after the recently dismissed President Compton. French had gathered faculty together to work through the situation harmoniously, much to everyone's surprise. It set the tone for his presidency: communication and transparency to heal division, all in the name of furthering the purpose of higher education. He often referred to himself as the April Fools' president, since he started work on April 1, and that further cemented his reputation as accessible, humble, and socially engaging. Yet, clearly, French was no fool when it came to leading Washington State to new heights.

THE PRIMARY THEMES OF FRENCH'S TENURE WERE growth and impact. The May 24, 1966, issue of the *Daily Evergreen*, which honored French with a front-page color photo, reported staggering information: "When Dr. French arrived on campus in the spring semester of 1952, the enrollment was 4,550 and there were 350 graduate students. Today there are 9,469 regularly enrolled students and 1,113 graduate students." The *Daily Evergreen* also emphasized the physical growth of the campus as well: "The total square footage of buildings on campus is 3,826,931, and of this figure, 2,270,490 has been built since Dr. French accepted the presidency."

Yet he was principled in ensuring that growth happened for the proper reasons. He explained this vision in a July 3, 1966, article in the *Spokesman-Review*: "quantitative growth would be a poor monument to leave behind. Most significant, I think, is the fact that this institution has changed from a college to a good, or better-than-good, university. I would be opposed to growth for the sake of growth." Four specific actions exemplify the qualitative growth at Washington State during French's tenure as its president. The most prominent was the transition to university status in 1959, the result of many years of expansion and growth on campus.

The predicted decline in enrollment in the early 1950s never happened; instead, enrollment continued to increase after French's arrival. Thanks to his never-tiring efforts in legislative lobbying, the school saw budget increases which helped improve faculty salaries. This, in turn, enabled WSC to attract interest from highly respected faculty across the country, which improved quality of instruction and research on campus. True to nature, French was not convinced in the mid-1950s the name change was appropriate or even necessary. The evolution from state college to state university would have to be initiated from the outside, from those recognizing the impact Washington State was having on the community and the state of Washington.

By 1957 increases in both faculty and student population mandated more physical space in Pullman. Washington voters soon approved a bond measure for construction at WSC, which provided the funding to build on campus and accommodate new needs. One year later, the Washington state senate introduced a bill to approve the campus for university status. The momentum in Pullman was undeniable, and the impact of French's administration on the growth of the college was beyond question. Much of this growth was academic, as Washington State now offered a wide array of undergraduate and graduate degrees far beyond its land-grant institution roots.

Helen and C. Clement French, 58th General Convention of the Episcopal Church, in Honolulu, Hawaii, September 1955. *C. Clement French Papers, cg310b2f09. WSU MASC.*

This pleased French, as he firmly believed in the role of education when it came to America, democracy, and the future of the country. In a written piece titled "Why You Should Read a Newspaper Every Day . . . ," appearing in print at the end of 1959, he argued, "We face a time of crisis in our affairs rarely, if ever, equaled in our history. Certainly not since the days of Thomas Paine, at least, has America needed to any greater extent the support of thoughtful citizen readers." As French saw it, the job of the entire educational system—and his campus in Pullman—was to develop those thoughtful citizen readers, so they could bolster and preserve the American way of life from outside threats to its security and sovereignty. French brought that vision to Pullman in a time of potential turmoil, and he led the school to university status.

Since Washington State College was far removed geographically from the political heart of the state in Olympia, French had done well cultivating relationships with both politicians and that other academic institution: the University of Washington. French's manner, communication style, and moral vision made both these tasks relatively manageable, despite differences and egos inherently present in such situations. An April 9, 1955, *Spokane Chronicle* piece—part of an Associated Press series on outstanding Northwest personalities—entitled "President of State College Is 'Door-Is-Open' Type," cited three anonymous faculty members' comments: 1) "If he has any weakness it is in being too fair—he takes too much burden on his own shoulders"; 2) "His greatest strength and the principal reason for his popularity is his sincerity and personal integrity"; and 3) "Talking to him is like talking to anyone."

It is difficult to effectively lead a university campus without connecting—on any level—with the faculty. This is not to imply the faculty has immeasurable power, but both president and faculty are part of the leadership structure empowering the university to pursue its missions and goals. The acceptance of symbiotic nature and agreement to communicate both ways improve life for everyone in the equation, including the students—the true constituency that many presidents and faculty members sometimes forget. French knew this, and his cultivation of healthy working relationships with the faculty also extended to his relationships with all colleagues and peers when it came to achieving his moral vision. State politicians were his colleagues; those at the University of Washington were his peers. These political and strategic relationships, built in earnest following his arrival in Pullman, were tremendously beneficial to the school.

Politics are pervasive in organizational leadership, and true leadership is in communication. A good leader needs to engage outside stakeholders effectively, too; situational insight helps a leader make the right decision for the specific moment at hand. Grasping implications and nuances is key to making the right decision, and often leadership is more about management and governance than administration. Successful higher education administration leaders rely on deft political leadership skills to manage crises when they arise. French did a great job making sure the crises did not arise, as he deftly handled situations with his approachable persona and effective communication skills illustrated by his open door and outreach to other stakeholders in situations he faced.

As result of the wavelength he had established carefully with the University of Washington, a nurtured relationship benefitting both institutions, the "rival" school actually helped sponsor the bill to initiate Washington State's name change in 1959. On the editorial page of the February 28, 1959, issue of the *Spokesman-Review*, French was lauded for his efforts, both public and private: "In actuality the school at Pullman has been a university for several years because of the wide range of its curriculum, its specialized instruction in various fields of learning and its activities and operations in areas other than the campus itself. By being identified officially as WSU, its prestige will be enhanced in this state and throughout the country. The way in which this change in name has been accomplished reflects credit upon President C. Clement French and the board of trustees."

This was the ultimate realization of French's moral vision for educational leadership: He had taken a smaller, land-grant institution and developed its potential for improving society through careful duty and guidance. He had not done it alone, of course, but French was the president, and in an era that was often defined by personal responsibility in leadership, he had delivered upon the promise of his hiring: WSC became Washington State University on September 1, 1959.

However, there was more significant growth to come for French and WSU. Pullman is isolated in the southeastern corner of the state, and it was only natural for the university to expand boundaries. The obvious location was Spokane, the largest metropolitan area in the east side of the state. Expanding WSU's academic footprint required more political maneuvering and more funds, though. That was no problem for French, now that the WSU brand was growing and thriving. Just a few years after the university achieved its new status, the possibility of a Spokane extension became a reality. It helped that the community of Spokane wanted a piece of Washington State University to call its own, as an editorial in the *Spokesman-Review* made clear on February 27, 1963:

> Washington State University's president, Dr. C. Clement French, did a good day's work for his institution in Spokane last Monday. He obtained consent of the city council for a lease to be drawn, between himself and the city manager, for the university's use of the large and well-built old building at Sprague and Cedar which the city library will abandon this spring. As this change may well lead to a considerable expansion of WSU activities in Spokane, both the city and the university's president are to be congratulated upon the decision. As Dr. French told the council, "This is a matter between two groups, both representing the public. I'm sure both the city and school will benefit." Of course, many in Spokane would like to see the whole campus moved closer to the city. Lacking that, the city would like very much to see more WSU activities here, both education and recreational.

It was inspired leadership to secure the beginning of a larger territorial footprint in higher education. The University of Washington putatively owned the west side of the state, thanks to its location in Seattle, the largest city in Washington and the site of the 1962 World's Fair—emphasizing its urban primacy in the Pacific Northwest. It made perfect sense for WSU to assert itself and its land-grant mission in the more rural, eastern side of the state. French's understanding of the university's need for expansion—for this was not growth for growth's sake—eventually led to the 1989 formalization by the state legislature of a branch campus in Spokane. Even though French left the presidency in 1966, WSU expansion was in large part due to the seed French planted during his time in Pullman.

Perhaps the least known element of WSU's growth and outreach is the international road French paved as president. The WSU Pakistan Project at the University of Punjab occurred during French's tenure, and in fall 1970, four years after his retirement, French completed *A Report of Washington State University's Participation in the Development of Institutions of Higher Learning in West Pakistan, 1954–1969.* This represented a global extension of French's vision for education. Pakistan remains the only modern nation to be created for the Islamic faith, and after its violent birth in 1947, the country needed what any nation would have needed in that time of crisis: assistance.

Perhaps a postcolonial analysis of these events might disagree with French's intentions, but higher education's role in the betterment of *any* society—core to his personal and professional moral vision as a leader—needs no revision. What worked for Washington State under French's visionary leadership worked for a new nation trying to establish itself in the modern world. In a September 9, 1963, *Spokesman-Review* piece, he wrote: "The availability to practically any young person who can profit from the opportunity for post–high school education is the heart of the unique American educational system. Society has realized that, through the support of this kind of system, the society itself is advanced. The progress of a democracy depends essentially upon the education of its citizens and their ability to choose."

Similar to the sentiment of his high-school graduation address forty-five years earlier, French saw a nation facing potential political chaos and in need of refined higher education practices to preserve itself from internal and external threats. It must have seemed very natural for him to pursue the opportunity in Pakistan, while also building international name recognition for the institute he presided over in the United States.

THE FOURTH AND FINAL NOTABLE AREA OF SIGNIFICANT growth during French's tenure at WSU was athletics. He once said, "Football is an interesting sideline. The primary function is not a good football team, but then we can't be too 'ivory-towerish' about it, either. We are in a tough conference, and we are mindful that every other sport on campus loses money. If it were not for our football team, then, these other athletes could not even compete." He clearly saw athletics as a part of the education experience, in terms of his moral philosophy. French

C. Clement and Helen French,
Taxila Excavation, Pakistan, March 1964.
C. Clement French Papers, cg310b2f14. WSU MASC.

knew athletic drive itself was important, and to deny the opportunity
for students to compete would be a violation of his vision as an educator.

While French did not cross paths with the legendary Bear Bryant
at Texas A&M—his two seasons in College Station were 1951–52, and
Bryant did not arrive until 1954—certainly he understood the power of
a good, competitive team. The Aggies were in the notorious (and now
defunct) Southwest Conference, a brutally competitive league in the
annals of college football history. When French arrived at Washington
State, the Cougars football team had not played in a bowl game since the

1930 season, losing the Rose Bowl to Alabama on January 1, 1931. WSU would not reach another bowl game until the 1981 season, long after his retirement. However, French did navigate the school's way through some tumultuous times as college athletics overall began to expand and proliferate in financial and political ways hitherto unimaginable.

Washington State was an early member of the Pacific Coast Conference, dating back to 1917. By 1958, though, the nine-school alliance was no longer tenable. Under-the-table money scandals in athletics at the University of Washington and three other PCC schools all but ended the conference's existence in spring 1959. In the November 4, 1966, edition of the *Spokesman-Review*, French's impact on WSU athletics was emphasized: "He followed the PCC code to the letter, though the very breakup of the PCC had been created by those who did not, and though WSU's leadership in efforts to compromise the troubles had availed to nothing. Through some awfully stormy times, Dr. French always impressed you with the calmness of his guidance. Looking back, you know it was only brilliance."

This is another moment when Kant's philosophy coincided with French's vision. To Kant, morality was the ultimate purpose for existence; nothing was more important or higher in the universe. And it all could collapse if just one beam of an individual's—or an organization's—moral house crashed to the ground. French was not willing to skirt rules and regulations to win, but he also wanted those athletic, character-building opportunities for WSU students. When five PCC schools formed the new Athletic Association of Western Universities in 1959, Washington State was not invited to join them. However, by 1962, the Cougars became the sixth team in what we now know today as the Pacific-12 Conference. French never compromised institutional integrity for the sake of athletics, although he did believe in athletics as an integral part of the higher education experience and fought for the preservation of WSU's sports programs.

French's leadership reaped long-term rewards, as the Cougars now field 17 men's and women's athletic teams in NCAA competition.

Without French's steady duty and resolve, it is possible the Cougars could have suffered the same fate as the neighboring University of Idaho Vandals, the ninth member of the PCC, that never made the leap to the AAWU. Every time ESPN's *College GameDay* airs and the WSU flag flies in the background, Cougar alumni can thank French for being who he was and preserving the WSU athletic program while also providing it the chance to grow with its old PCC rivals in a stronger conference.

THE 1960S FEATURED CONTINUED TREMENDOUS GROWTH for Washington State. As the faculty on campus improved, so did the opportunities for students—and more of them came to WSU than ever before in history. Yet it was the moments like commencement ceremonies that really endeared French to the students in Pullman. His practicality and deference to them in respectful moments was well known. Before one spring commencement, for example, French told the media in advance, "They have me listed on the program, but I'm not making a speech. Many of the seniors want to leave for home as early as they can Sunday afternoon, and I'm not going to delay them."

Although lighthearted in nature, French always cared about his students, and he demonstrated this by continually passing on his moral philosophy and wisdom to them at commencement time. In some ways, these words were his greatest gift to a generation of college students who would go on to accomplish great things. French encapsulated this vision in his 1965 commencement address: "And so the university, in its concern for both the preservation of what has been and the development of what is to be, has the very difficult responsibility in the world today of conserving the past and looking to the future. That will not be helped, in my opinion, if those of you who have become better able to live in the days ahead by having been here do not accept as you go out today your responsibility for the furtherance and the advancement and the proper changing, if you will, of the nature of this institution."

C. Clement French
at his final WSU
commencement,
May 1966.
*C. Clement French
Papers, cg31ob3f18.
WSU MASC.*

Some notable students that graduated during French's presidency
include sports commentator Keith Jackson (1954), Space Shuttle astro-
naut John M. Fabian (1962), Washington governor Mike Lowry (1962),
and noted educator Laurence J. Peter, namesake of the Peter Principle,
who completed his doctoral studies in education at WSU in 1963. Of
course, French impacted many students during his 14 years in the presidency, including thousands of graduates that have improved lives in
their communities after receiving their education at the state's land-grant
institution—both in fulfillment of the university's mission and French's
moral vision of education.

One of those students was his own son. In 1954, French had the honor
of handing a bachelor's degree to his son Richard during graduation—the

first WSU president to do so. Richard went on to attend Wycliffe Hall at Oxford, earning a certificate there in 1957. The vision French touted as an administrator did not get lost on his children, and in many ways, he was a parental figure to the thousands of Washington State graduates that crossed paths with him in Pullman from 1952 to 1966, each of them fulfilling their duty and obligation to WSU.

WHEN FRENCH CHOSE TO RETIRE IN 1966 AS HE TURNED 65, he did so with just as little fanfare as when he arrived. As the story goes, he always told everyone he started on April Fools' Day, left on Halloween, and was never inaugurated. His impact upon the university was too significant to let his retirement go unnoticed and uncelebrated, however.

A July 3, 1966, article in the *Spokesman-Review* glowed about him: "At his inauguration, Dr. C. Clement French warned the graduating seniors 'to put no faith in magic; learn that there are really no rabbits in hats.' Yet it in the 14 years that followed, it would seem that some form of magic descended upon the campus in the Palouse to transform it from what Seattleites called a 'cow college' to a major institution of learning in the Pacific Northwest." That was the kind of growth French savored in his vision of educational leadership. At the same time, he was never one to accept sole honors for any achievement. In the September 23, 1966, edition of the *WSU News Bulletin*, French wrote some parting words: "To each of you, in this final statement to my colleagues, I repeat my deep appreciation for all you have done to further the progress of the university during the years of my Presidency."

As the fall rolled around, the date of French's retirement grew closer. In the game program for the Oregon State–Washington State home football game on October 29, 1966, there was a special farewell for French: "Coming to WSU on April 1, 1952, the greatest transformation in the university's history has occurred during Dr. French's 14-plus years at the helm. To Dr. French and his lovely wife, Helen, we say thank

Helen and C. Clement
French at alumni board
meeting in La Conner,
Washington, August 27,
1966. WSU Reports, *Fall
1966, pg. 2. WSU MASC.*

you for a job well done and for selecting Pullman as a permanent home
during retirement days." Two days later, French officially stepped down
as the president of Washington State University. He had joked in the
Spokesman-Review article over the summer that, "It is best to leave while
they are asking me to stay. Better that way than to have old friends come
back to campus later on say, 'My gosh, are you still here?'"

One of the best legacies a campus president can leave behind is a
namesake building, and it came in the form of the French Administration Building. Dedicated on April 27, 1968, the current description notes
the building "holds offices for university administrators and student
services, including the president, human resources and personnel, the
registrar, the dean of student affairs, equity and diversity, and more.

French Ad is joined to the Lighty Student Services Building; with each building's hallways flowing seamlessly into the next, they function together as a central home for administration and student support."

That is what French wanted: a seamless functioning home for everyone on campus so they could fulfill their duty to society. The April 27, 1968, building dedication program stated that French retired "as one of the nation's most distinguished educators." In his dedication remarks, Dr. H. H. Hahner—the president of the Board of Regents at the time—quoted a Spokane newspaper editorial: "The people of the Inland Empire and the State of Washington will always owe a debt of gratitude to Dr. C. Clement French who has done such a magnificent job for Washington State University."

ON NOVEMBER 1, 1966, FRENCH WAS NAMED PRESIDENT emeritus at Washington State University, and his retirement began in earnest as he and Helen established the C. Clement and Helen B. French Scholarship at WSU. One noticeable change on campus was the absence of his green cars. French was famous for always choosing a green car, and he explained why the summer before his retirement: "I had my reasons for the green cars. I have a habit of parking illegally on the campus sometimes, and I wanted the campus police to know right off whose car it was in front of a fire plug." Needless to say, the campus police missed writing those tickets.

The Frenches had planned to travel once official WSU duties were completed, but Helen experienced some health problems which delayed those intentions. While French received offers to do many things in his post-presidency days, he was quite selective in how he spent his time. In May 1968, French turned down the position of chair of the study committee for the Investigation of the Scientific Aspects of Veterinary Medical Research and Education at the National Academy of Sciences for the National Research Council. This was the most notable of many offers French declined upon his completion of service to WSU, and it demonstrated the high esteem in which he was held for his efforts at Washington State over 14 years.

French did choose to be on the Constitutional Revision Commission for the State of Washington under Governor Daniel J. Evans. As the chair of the commission, French submitted the final report to the governor on June 17, 1969. Evans' thank-you note to French on October 24, 1969, noted, "I believe it is the most significant document on constitutional reform ever published in our state and should serve as a guideline for future constitutional revision by the legislature and the people." A 1968 summer feature in the *Daily Evergreen* once more affirmed French's sense of humor: "I tried to tell Dan that the Regents hadn't really fired me and that I wasn't looking for a job, but he twisted my arm at the shoulder, so that I had to give in and accept."

As the 1970s began, French and his wife made good on a promise to be silent spectators in Pullman. Helen died in 1976, and French passed away 12 years later. He was 86 years old, his life having spanned the majority of the twentieth century and all the changes it wrought on America, democracy, and the world. French remained constant throughout it all, much to the benefit of Washington State University and all those who walked its grounds from 1952 to 1966 while French guided the campus through its most prominent stage of ascent.

DR. M. CECIL MACKEY, FORMER PRESIDENT AT SOUTH Florida, Texas Tech, and Michigan State universities in the 1970s and 1980s, once noted that, "Colleges and universities in general are institutions for which the public has respect. Maintaining an operation whose policies and practices produce a continuing flow of high-profile scandal is a great disservice both to the individual institution involved and to the public's general perception of colleges and universities." Thanks to C. Clement French, the 1952–1966 era for Washington State University maintained and increased public respect after the challenging times that had come before French's tenure, without a trace of scandal. He handled all the requisite challenges at WSU with dignity and aplomb.

Adam Smith wrote, "The administration of the great system of the universe . . . the care of the universal happiness of all rational and sensible beings, is the business of God and not of man. To man is allotted a much humbler department, but one much more suitable to the weakness of his powers, and to the narrowness of his comprehension: the care of his own happiness, of that of his family, his friends, his country." French's faith, developed in his youth as a strong influence on his moral vision for not only his own life but for those he impacted as well, carried him to great heights as the president of Washington State University. French's sense of duty, forged in the shadow of global conflict and turmoil, is why WSU still remembers him with such admiration and respect.

Washington State Magazine summarized it well, almost twenty years after French's passing, in its summer 2007 issue: "That is the kind of leader he was—one with a great sense of humor, a sincere appreciation of the value of every employee, great organizational abilities, and tremendous sense of fairness. He always emphasized the importance of each individual in the particular job he or she had at the University."

RESEARCH NOTES

The Charles Clement French Papers, 1914–1971, housed in the Manuscripts, Archives, and Special Collections (MASC) at the Washington State University Libraries, established the basis for much of this biography. In addition, the accompanying photos all come from MASC. A May 1983 interview with French, preserved in the MASC oral history archive, was instrumental as well.

The archives of the WSU student paper, the *Daily Evergreen*, contributed significantly, as well, in terms of providing student perspective on French's tenure as president. Local city and community newspapers in Pullman and Spokane provided public viewpoints throughout his presidency. Various web resources at WSU helped flesh out the narrative, too, including Gen De Vleming's 2007 contribution to the *Washington State Magazine* focused on WSU presidents.

Finally, the analytical frameworks for this biography of an academic leader originated in the author's doctoral studies and writings on organizational leadership in higher education at Michigan State University (2006–2014), under the collective guidance of Dr. Marilyn Amey, Dr. Marylee Davis, and Dr. Cecil Mackey.

Any specific inquiries as to the information and sources used for this narrative can be directed to the author, who kept detailed notes during the research process for this writing.

W. Glenn Terrell
1967–1985

BY JOHN TAPPAN MENARD

*I*N THE LATE 1960S AND EARLY '70S, PROTESTS, VIOLENCE, and strife wracked college campuses across the nation. At their worst, these protests became lethal, perhaps best embodied by the infamous killings at Kent State University and Jackson State University. While at times Pullman, Washington, can feel insulated from the struggles gripping the nation as a whole, in the late '60s Washington State University's campus experienced the anti-war and civil rights movements. In times of strife, it takes a steady hand of leadership to steer an institution, and in the age of civil rights and the Vietnam War, President Glenn Terrell provided that hand.

William Glenn Terrell was born May 24, 1920, in Tallahassee, Florida, into a well-educated family. His father (also William Glenn Terrell) served as a justice on the Florida Supreme Court for a record forty-one years. Young Glenn Terrell attended Davidson College for his undergraduate degree and was an active member of the college's ROTC program. After the Japanese attack on Pearl Harbor, the army assigned Terrell to the 30th Infantry Division, then later transferred him to the Headquarters Division of the U.S. VII Corps. As part of the VII Corps, Terrell waded ashore at Utah Beach on June 6, 1944, during the Allied invasion

Terrell poses for a photo during
his inauguration on July 1, 1967.
*Historic WSU Photographs
Collection, pc004b35bf06.
WSU MASC.*

of Normandy. He later participated in the liberation of Paris, and saw
combat in the Battle of the Bulge. Upon his discharge from the army,
Terrell had proven himself a capable leader—a trait which earned him
commendation from his superiors—and left the service having achieved
the rank of captain. After the war, Terrell returned to his education,
earning a master's degree in psychology from Florida State University
and his doctoral degree in developmental psychology from the University of Iowa. Terrell quickly developed an impressive academic resume,
serving as the chair of the Psychology Department at the University of
Colorado, then later became the dean of the College of Liberal Arts and
the dean of Faculties at the University of Illinois–Chicago.

When the regents of Washington State University expressed interest
in Terrell as a candidate for president, Terrell, perhaps inadvertently, did
everything in his power to reject their overtures. Fate, it seems, had other
plans. Terrell visited the campus in late 1965. Though he found Pullman
and WSU charming, he expressed reservations about the remoteness of

the university and of giving up his teaching duties for administrative ones. When the regents offered Terrell the presidency, he declined. Undeterred, the regents talked Terrell into making another visit to campus. Terrell agreed, but he had scarcely boarded the plane to Spokane before he changed his mind. Terrell exited the plane, and informed the regents that he did not wish to accept their offer. That should have been the end of it, but WSU wanted Terrell, even if Terrell did not yet want WSU. Some eight months later, the regents contacted Terrell yet again, once again offering him the presidency. Time, and a particularly brutal Chicago winter, had warmed Terrell to the idea of being president. He accepted, and on July 1, 1967, interim president Wallis Beasley handed over the reins to W. Glenn Terrell, who became the seventh president of Washington State University. Terrell began his tenure with an ample $40,000 a year salary, and the regents approved the spending of $200,000 in renovations to the President's Mansion, including the addition of a two car garage.

THOUGH TERRELL NEVER PUBLICLY EXPRESSED ANY regret for having taken the job, the start of his presidency was not an easy one. The late '60s were turbulent times. The war in Vietnam raged endlessly; Martin Luther King Jr. fell to an assassin's bullet in Memphis, Tennessee, as did Robert Kennedy in California. Protestors clashed with police at the Democratic National Convention in Chicago; the Black Panthers occupied the California state capitol building and policed the streets of Oakland; hippies practiced free love and celebrated the Age of Aquarius at love-ins and in the fields of Woodstock. The blooming counterculture raged against the silent majority.

One of the biggest issues facing Terrell at the start of his presidency was the campus's racial climate. Racist incidents of varying severity were common at WSU, particularly against black students, but other minority groups were also targeted. Two episodes gripped the attention of the community in particular at the start of Terrell's presidency. The first was an incident involving black students from Garfield High School in Seattle who were bussed to Pullman for a campus visit in May 1968. They had expected to attend a dance at Stephenson Hall, but no dance happened and they were asked to leave. The students then gathered on the lawn outside Rogers Hall, where they were subjected to multiple racial slurs from WSU students and had objects thrown at them from the dormitory windows. In the second incident, the student-run newspaper, the *Evergreen*, published a satirical story in the vein of George Orwell's *Animal Farm,* which depicted black students as literal "sheep" attempting to violently take over a barnyard inhabited by white "cows," stirring further outrage. Additionally, letters to the editor published by the *Evergreen* at that time frequently included use of the epithet "nigger" in reference to black students. Needless to say, the climate for black students at WSU, of which there were less than 100, was not very welcoming in the late '60s. Terrell proved a very vocal critic of racism, and his experiences in World War II left him similarly disposed toward violence. "I cannot think of more serious illnesses of a society than racism and war," he wrote in his memoir. Terrell endeavored to back up his words with action, significantly expanding the institutional apparatus of WSU to handle issues of discrimination during his tenure.

Challenges came early for the new president. In January 1969, less than a year after the Garfield High School incident, racial tensions flared up on campus. Despite the cold weather, on January 9 tempers ran hot between members of two intramural basketball teams. During a supposedly friendly match between the mixed-race team from the Goldsworthy dormitory and the all-white team from the Alpha Gamma Rho fraternity, the game quickly devolved into pushing and shoving. Amidst the scrum, the two teams exchanged heated words, which reportedly contained the epithet "black bastard" directed toward one member of the Goldsworthy team. (It should be noted that accounts of this incident and subsequent events vary widely in the finer details). The referees broke the two teams apart, and they departed without further incident. But the issue festered. A few days later, on January 15, witnesses reported seeing somewhere between ten and twenty black students entering the AGR house shortly before 11 p.m., some of them armed with rifles and pipes. A confrontation ensued inside the house and several weapons were discharged, resulting in significant property damage to the house. Five members of AGR suffered minor injuries, though none from gunfire, and were treated at the local hospital. Civil authorities and WSU both launched independent investigations into the incident and ultimately six black WSU students were arrested in the aftermath of the fight, including Ernie Thomas, then head of the Black Student Union.

The exact sequence of events leading up to the brawl at the AGR house remained a matter of great contention, with both sides blaming each other for instigating it. According to the Black Student Union, on the day of the brawl a female member of the BSU working the phones at the BSU's office received a phone call from a member of AGR. The AGR member allegedly told her that BSU representatives and the Goldsworthy team were welcome to go to the AGR house to discuss the incident, but warned that the AGRs were also "ready for any other kind of action." Eddie Leon, who would become president of the BSU following the arrest of Thomas, further claimed the fraternity member also told the woman that the AGRs would have guns present at the meeting. This, the BSU asserted, was their impetus for bringing firearms to the meeting. BSU leadership addressed the contents of the phone call in a meeting held later that day, where they decided that members of the team and the BSU would accept the AGRs invitation to meet them at the house.

The members of AGR, however, recounted a much different version of events. AGR representatives flatly denied that any member of AGR had ever placed a phone call to the BSU's office and also denied any use of firearms by house members. In an official statement released shortly after the incident, AGR offered this version of events: "The house president came out from the kitchen; saw a Negro standing on a table and asked him to get off. The house president was then physically assaulted along with other AGRs who were in the area. . . . Shots were fired by the Negroes both inside the house and from outside the house. One witness counted six shots." The AGRs remained steadfast in their insistence that the BSU bore responsibility for the violence, while the BSU alleged the opposite. The police never pursued any legal action against the AGRs.

Whatever the actual facts, the fallout quickly engulfed the Palouse. Furor from black and white students alike coursed across campus. Angry letters from both sides flowed into the columns of the *Evergreen* and Terrell's office was inundated daily with calls from concerned parents. The BSU quickly challenged what they perceived as racial discrimination on part of the police: why were only black students facing criminal charges and not any members of AGR? In a statement published in the *Evergreen*, the BSU declared their support for the accused students: "We fully and unconditionally support our brothers in the current struggle. We deplore the divided attention towards our black brothers and demand that equal time be directed towards the AGR Fraternity. Only the brothers are to appear before the [university's] disciplinary board. Only the brothers are charged with felinous [*sic*] assault. Only the brothers are attacked by rumor and invidious slander. Only the brothers are assumed guilty." These were not just cheap words. The BSU later proved that some of them, quite literally, were willing to die for their fellow black students.

Of the six students charged, two plead guilty to second-degree assault and were sentenced to 90 days in jail and three years of probation, and three plead guilty to third-degree assault and received 30 day sentences and one year of probation (the charges against the sixth student were later dropped). Superior Court Judge John A. Denoo allowed the students to serve their sentences on weekends so that they could continue to attend classes at WSU. When it came time for the men to serve their first weekend in jail though, events did not proceed smoothly. On Thursday, February 27, 1969, the Black Student Union issued four "non-negotiable" demands to Terrell. In the statement, as reported in the *Evergreen*, the BSU asked Terrell to use his power as university president to lobby the judicial system to suspend the sentences of the convicted students, to suspend the university disciplinary committee's investigations of the students, to promise that no disciplinary action would be taken toward any faculty, student, or staff who openly supported the students, and to grant academic leave to the convicted students and any of their supporters who desired it. The BSU set a deadline of 4:00 p.m. on Friday, February 28, for Terrell to respond to their demands, otherwise they promised to "use any means necessary

Terrell examines an historic American flag (42 stars) with history professor David Stratton, 1977. *Historic WSU Photographs Collection, pc004b35b. WSU MASC.*

to rectify these grave injustices." Despite the strong words, Terrell rejected all of the BSU's demands, noting, among other things, that he had no power to intercede in the functions of the judicial system.

Terrell's response came too late to meet the deadline, and members of the BSU and other sympathetic activists rallied to make good on their warning. Led by WSU professor Johnnetta Cole, a group of roughly sixty protestors gathered in front of the courthouse in Colfax and surrounded the convicted students upon their arrival with the county sheriffs, preventing them from entering the courthouse. County Sheriff Mike Humphries tried to get the group to disperse, but they refused, telling Humphries that he would have to arrest them all. A lack of space in the jail prevented Humphries from jailing the entire group. The situation took a turn for the worse as a counter-protest consisting primarily of residents from Colfax formed to protest the protestors. The two sides jeered at each other, and several rocks were thrown at the courthouse, breaking three windows—though which side they came from is unknown. Tensions rose to a breaking point, and law enforcement officers from as far as Spokane raced to Colfax in anticipation of a violent end to the standoff.

Looking for assistance, Professor Cole telephoned Terrell's office in Pullman, explaining that the situation was fast getting out of hand. Terrell consulted with Sheriff Humphries over the phone. Together, the three, along with a sympathetic Episcopal priest, devised a plan in which the protestors, under the escort of the police, moved to the safety of the priest's church to escape the counter-protestors. There they stayed the night, surrounded by law enforcement. Terrell and his office stayed in constant contact with authorities during the standoff. Several WSU employees arrived from Pullman to provide the protestors with hamburgers, drinks, and blankets to help them make it through the night. Fear and uncertainty coursed amongst the protestors as rumors circulated that an armed mob of vigilante farmers was assembling to kill them. Numerous protestors had brought firearms with them, and thus prepared to risk their lives in a potential shootout.

Fortunately, the night passed without incident, and the next morning the priest asked the protestors to leave the church, as he had received violent threats from local residents. After returning to the courthouse and negotiating further with Humphries, the protestors moved again to take shelter in a Catholic church. At 1:30 p.m. on March 1, the remaining forty-two protestors submitted peacefully to arrest. The five convicted students were brought back into custody and began to serve their sentences. What could have been a tragic and violent racial incident ended peacefully. Sheriff Humphries received high praise from Terrell and the BSU for avoiding any bloodshed during the standoff. The BSU sent Sheriff Humphries a dozen roses as thanks, which Terrell described as one of the most touching student gestures he witnessed during his tenure. Washington Governor Dan Evans also praised Humphries and WSU administration for their handling of the incident.

More potential trouble loomed, however. The findings of the university's disciplinary investigation were still pending. The convicted students faced possible expulsion from school in addition to their jail sentences. Rumors circulated that a scene similar to the one in Colfax could break out on campus if the Discipline Committee ruled harshly against the students. The campus waited breathlessly for the committee's decision, which was to be handed down on March 5. Shortly before the committee was set to announce their decision, Terrell released an open letter to the WSU community which stated that disciplinary action against the five students was suspended indefinitely—but that this decision was contingent on the full cooperation of the students with the court's sentence, and that no more demonstrations relating to the incident be held. The pragmatic decision by Terrell quelled any serious additional unrest relating to the AGR incident.

THE NEXT SCHOOL YEAR WOULD PROVIDE TERRELL WITH HIS greatest test. The spring of 1970 saw more strife, for both the country and the Palouse. Incidents in March and April on campus, including the arson of the south stands of the football field, and the arrest of four black students for the rape of a white woman (two of the students were ultimately convicted), created a tense and ugly mood on campus. However, the discontent surrounding these issues was a mere warm-up for the events that followed. Few months can claim to be more tumultuous for the United States and Pullman than May 1970. The unrest began on April 30, when President Nixon announced the invasion of Cambodia. Protests erupted across the country. On May 4 National Guard members killed four and wounded twelve demonstrators against the Cambodian invasion at Kent State University in Ohio. On the Palouse, in the early morning hours of May 5, a University of Idaho student and Marine recently returned from Vietnam firebombed the National Guard armory in Lewiston, resulting in the destruction of several dozen vehicles. That same day, an arsonist firebombed the Navy ROTC building on the UI campus.

Only twelve hours after the attack on the Lewiston armory, the nation's collective outrage manifested itself in Pullman; just after noon between 500 and 800 WSU students occupied the French Administration Building (derisively called "Fort French" by student activists) to protest the war in Cambodia and the Kent State shootings. President Terrell was not in Pullman at the time of the sit-in, but was scheduled to fly in later that day. Upon his arrival, Terrell rushed to the administration building, where he addressed the protestors. The conversation that followed was remarkable. While indignant, the protesting students listened quietly as Terrell spoke, punctuating Terrell's speech with raucous cheers when they agreed with him and a torrent of boos when they did not.

The students demanded that Terrell cancel classes on Thursday in order to hold a teach-in on Southeast Asia. Students also called on Terrell to send a telegram to President Nixon, denouncing—on the behalf of the university—the invasion of Cambodia. Terrell indicated he was willing to send Nixon a telegram, but he argued he could not speak for the university as a whole. Over the course of an hour, Terrell and the students went back and forth over the particulars of the telegram. Terrell came up with a draft that satisfied the students, and after an informal vote, the protestors accepted the draft and began to clean up French Administration, taking care to leave it exactly as they found it, "except more enlightened" one student joked. Victorious, many of the protestors headed to the Compton Union Building to celebrate their triumph. The occupation of "Fort French" was over after only nine hours, without bloodshed or violence, a striking but welcome difference from similar events playing out across the country. Terrell's official telegram to Nixon stated, in part:

> The recent events on the campus of Kent State University and the extension of the war into Cambodia have created outrage and dismay on the part of a substantial segment of the campus at Washington State University. You have observed similar reactions across the nation. Many on our campus deplore the decision to send troops into Cambodia and the tragic death of the four students at Kent State.

Nola Cross (center, in white), *Evergreen* journalist, observes an anti-draft protest in Pullman, March 13, 1970. *Paul Philemon Kies Photographs, pc028b16_70b17_19700313. WSU MASC.*

While Terrell may have satisfied some of the student protestors, he upset many faculty, alumni, and politicians across the state of Washington. Letters, some measured in their criticisms, some brimming with fury, began to rush in. Terrell's secretary, Gen DeVleming, estimates that they received over 1,000 letters. Terrell or his executive vice president, Wallis Beasley, personally replied to every letter but one, which Terrell described as "too ugly to deserve an answer." Other alumni chose to voice their anger and frustration indirectly via letters to the editor of the university's alumni magazine, *Hilltopics*, or to regent's president Harold Romberg.

WSU faculty and staff were among the first to express their discontent. A May 7 letter to Romberg signed by sixty-two WSU employees aired their grievances. "A President of a University should represent ALL the students . . . it is a sad day when 800 students and a President can attempt to speak for 13,000," they wrote. "[M]ore than any time in history, the students need to have figures of strength looming before them. We need to have authority before us, not acquiescence. . . . President

Terrell gave in . . . [b]y giving in to these spoiled children's demands we are reinforcing their behavior instead of stopping it. Such behavior cannot be tolerated . . . or soon we will have anarchy, anarchy that was born and bred in the University. Where will our freedom be then?"

State Representative James P. Kuehle, in a letter to Terrell, expressed disappointment that Terrell had "capitulated" to a "minority group" on campus. According to Kuehle, the situation on Washington's college campuses was far past "the point where we must eliminate from university staffs another minority group of leftists and anarchists." The situation was so dire to Kuehle he threatened to call a special session of the state legislature to eliminate tenure for professors, and even perhaps shut down state universities "until such a time a proper academic atmosphere can be restored."

The letters to *Hilltopics* were similarly critical, though some alumni voiced their support. Douglas P. Salisbury ('40) blasted Terrell for giving in to "500 wine-sipping, cheese-chewing students." Another, Air Force General Delmar Edmond Wilson ('36) opined, "I consider it completely revolting when 500 – 800 students, regardless of color or creed, can dictate the environment for an enrollment of 13,000." Others came to the defense of the embattled president. "President Terrell is being crucified for circumstances he has no means of controlling," wrote Marjorie Anderson ('50) of Portland, Oregon, to *Hilltopics*. A sympathetic onlooker, Francis Butler, wrote to Terrell directly: "Dear Dr. Terrell, I have not worried about your recent decisions because I've had great faith in your judgement and experience. I'm sure the past weeks have given you a deep appreciation of the Harry Truman slogan 'The Buck Stops Here'."

Unrest continued locally and nationally. On May 8, construction workers in New York City clashed violently with student protestors. Over seventy people suffered injuries during the fracas, which became known as the "Hard-Hat Riot." On May 14, police shot and killed two black students and injured twelve others at Jackson State University. On May 15, during a review of the WSU ROTC at Rogers Field, protestors disrupted the proceedings, ostensibly throwing butchered animal meat in front of the cadets as they marched by Terrell and other university officials. Several protestors also saw fit to give Terrell the Nazi salute accompanied by shouts of "Sieg Heil!"

The biggest event of May came three days later. The upheaval on campus and across the country deeply troubled student activists. In particular, the killings at Jackson State prompted black student activists to call WSU's various activist organizations together at the Koinonia House to address issues of race on campus. The racially charged incidents taking place across campus and the country had to end, they felt. Though the students could not stamp out racism in America overnight, they felt they could affect substantive change at WSU. It was agreed that the students would present a list of demands to President Terrell that were designed to combat the systemic racism present in the university system, as well as ease the hostile racial climate on WSU's campus. A general student strike would back up the demands. Thus, the ensuing student strike of May 1970 was not, as is popularly remembered, a strike against the war in Vietnam and Cambodia, but a strike against racism. On May 18, 1970, less than two weeks after the occupation of French Administration, members of the Black Student Union, El Movimiento Estudiantil Chicano/a Atzlan (MEChA), the Radical Union (a successor to Students for a Democratic Society), the Three Forks Peace Coalition, the Young Socialist Alliance, and the Women's Liberation Front delivered a list of demands to Terrell, asking for change on campus. Below is a brief summary of some of their demands:

- The immediate disarmament of campus police and ROTC.
- The establishment of a review board to examine all law enforcement actions against minority students. (The strikers used the term "Third World" in place of minority.)
- Abolishment of the university's disciplinary board.
- Establishment of a Third World Review Board to work with the Publications Board in fighting racism on campus through student publications.
- A ten day mandatory racism workshop for all faculty and staff during the fall semester.
- Immediate efforts to bring minority enrollments in line with national demographics.

- Active financial and administrative support of the black studies program.
- Immediate removal of all non-union grapes from campus.

On May 22, Terrell responded to the student's demands, rejecting all
of them. Terrell expressed sympathy with the frustrations underlying the
demands. "I agree fully that we must wage a relentless struggle against
racial discrimination in American society generally on the campuses
of our colleges and universities," he wrote. However, he disagreed with
the assessment that the university was not doing enough to combat
racism. "I fail to understand the implication . . . that the university has
taken no steps to improve conditions for the minorities." Terrell then
cited some of the university's actions, including the establishment of
committees intended to help meet the needs of minority groups, the
newly launched Black Studies program, and the pending approval of
programs in Chicano Studies and Native American Studies. It should
be noted though that Terrell erroneously believed that the demands
were "non-negotiable," and that rejection of ultimatums was standard
practice at the time for university presidents across the country. Terrell's
assumption that the demands could not be negotiated was perhaps based
on the fact that previously issued demands from the BSU to him in the
AGR incident were explicitly couched as "non-negotiable." Nevertheless,
the strikers had not intended them to be interpreted that way.

As a riposte to Terrell's rejection, the BSU, MEChA, and the Radical Union called on the students of WSU to join them in a strike. That
afternoon, hundreds of protestors blocked off Stadium Way, the main
thoroughfare through campus. One protestor put a two-by-four through
the windshield of car—though some accounts claim that this act of
violence only occurred after the driver of the car threatened to run over
the students. The strike was on. Ultimately it is impossible to get an
accurate count of how many students participated in the strike, but there
were at least a few thousand participants. While many were motivated
to see the goals of the strike leaders carried out, other students merely
relished an opportunity to avoid classes. Strikers picketed regularly on
the Compton Union Building mall, held marches, boycotted classes,

distributed leaflets, and organized an economic boycott of Pullman businesses that did not publicly denounce racism. While the strike was calm, especially compared to other protests going on across the country, there were some violent incidents. An arsonist attempted to burn the rest of the football field's stands, one or more malcontents hurled rocks through the front windows of the student bookstore, a firebomb was discovered on campus, and bomb threats were so prevalent that some departments organized night watches to protect their offices from harm.

On Wednesday, May 27, several thousand students gathered in Bohler Gym. Among other points discussed, they agreed to march on French Administration and conduct a march through various classroom buildings that Friday. After the meeting, a crowd of between 2,000 and 3,000 students, some of them carrying make-shift torches, marched from Bohler to the president's house, demanding that Terrell address them. At 9 p.m., Terrell, with the aid of a portable amplifier, spoke to the students filling his front grass, the street, and the lawns of several nearby sororities. "If I did not love you all and believe in you all so much, I'd be scared," he told the students (though he later admitted in his memoir to being "just a little nervous" during the confrontation). Thanks to the help of some faculty sympathetic to the strike, who had privately explained the student's intentions to Terrell, he now knew that the demands presented to him were not "non-negotiable." With this new piece of information, and the urgent motivation that comes with having a mass of torch-welding students on your lawn, Terrell agreed to meet with strike representatives the next morning in order to discuss ending the strike. The negotiating process proved tense, requiring several meetings, one of which ended with the striker's delegation walking out on Terrell after two hours of negotiations. At last, on June 1, Terrell and his administration, along with representatives of BSU and MEChA, announced that the strike had ended. Multiple changes were implemented by WSU administration to end the strike. Among them:

- The appointment of a special assistant to the president. This assistant's responsibilities included the development of programs designed to combat racism, and to investigate instances of racial discrimination on campus and report findings to the president's office.

- The creation of an advisory council consisting of two black, two Chicano, and two Native American students, at the recommendation of their respective student organizations, to help the special assistant improve campus life for minority students.
- The creation of "Racism Workshops," which were to be held in lieu of classes for two days in the fall semester, and two in the following spring semester.
- Regular in-service trainings on racial discrimination for central administrative staff.
- The hiring of Chicano, black, and Native American students by the admissions office to assist in recruitment of minority groups.

Once again, Terrell's concession to student demands brought about a deluge of criticism from parents, alumni, and community members. The cancellation of classes to hold racism workshops was a particular point of discontent, though the fall workshops were ultimately very successful and drew over 20,000 people. A small group of alumni from Yakima, Washington, telegrammed Terrell with the sarcastic message: "[w]e are certainly glad that you spent tax payers money to promote two days of racism on your campus." An anonymous postcard, addressing Terrell as the "Great Masochist," called for Terrell to be institutionalized. The sender, utilizing a red sharpie, etched two misshapen swastikas onto the postcard to emphasize the point. Another alumnus wrote to *Hilltopics* and compared Terrell's negotiation with the strikers to British Prime Minister Neville Chamberlain's appeasement of Adolf Hitler.

Some faculty, too, were upset. In an anonymous letter to Terrell, dated June 1, six faculty members blasted Terrell over his handling of the strike. "Dr. Terrell, you have betrayed the faculty and the students of this University. . . . You have lost the faith and respect and the trust of the community of Pullman and of the . . . WSU alumni association as well. . . . You are actually the laughing stock in many conversations both on and off the campus. . . . We have heard it said that you actually believe that you are doing a good job. How unfortunate that you, a

The Terrell family: Francine (wife), Francie (daughter), and Glenn Terrell III (son) outside the president's mansion with dogs Vicki (white) and Sue (brown), ca. 1969–1970. *Historic WSU Photographs Collection, pc004b35b-terrellfamily2. WSU MASC.*

psychologist, can be so blind." The letter concluded, "Mr. Terrell, you are going to be a short term President. . . . We simply can not [*sic*] be loyal to a President with such poor administrative judgement."

Student reactions were mixed. Some were not satisfied with the agreement, while others were relieved that the strike had ended peacefully. Strikers and non-strikers alike were probably grateful that Terrell had announced that final exams would be optional for students, due to the stress that the preceding weeks had caused; however, many alumni were not pleased by this decision. What had proved an intense semester ended on a happy note at commencement that June, where the graduates gave Terrell a standing ovation.

THE REST OF TERRELL'S CAREER AS PRESIDENT CARRIED its fair share of challenges. Racial tensions flared up from time to time on campus, as they still do today. In 1979 students and staff of WSU's women's athletic programs sued the university for violation of Title IX. In the case, which became known as *Blair vs. Washington State University*, the plaintiffs alleged that WSU did not provide adequate funding for women's athletics. Terrell provided testimony in the Superior Court case, heard in 1982, and the State Supreme Court sided with the plaintiffs in 1987, ordering the university to adequately fund women's athletics. May 1980 also proved an exciting month. The eruption of Mount St. Helens inundated Pullman with ash, and Terrell faced the tough decision of whether or not to cancel classes once again. He did cancel classes for one day, and he and his staff spent the next week on the phones soothing anxious parents. Under Terrell, the university also accomplished a number of milestones. Minority enrollment nearly tripled, from 2.6 percent of the student population in 1968 to 7 percent in 1985 when Terrell retired. Additionally, WSU established its alumni association, helped start the WWAMI medical program, and swelled total enrollment from 11,000 in 1967 to 15,500 in 1985. Finally, Terrell secured a large donation for a new football stadium from alumnus Dan Martin, whose father, Clarence Martin, had served as the governor of Washington state. Because of the donation, the new facility was named Martin Stadium, in the governor's honor. However, Clarence Martin was also an alumnus of the University of Washington. So in an ironic twist, the WSU Cougars play in a stadium partly named after a Husky.

To Glenn Terrell fell the unenviable responsi-
bility of being in a position of leadership in the late '60s and early '70s.
As president, he was caught up in one of the largest cultural shifts the
United States has ever seen. On one hand, he had to contend with the
traditionalist views of state legislators, alumni, regents, and parents,
while on the other hand he had to be attentive to the needs and ideals of
a significant block within the baby boomer generation, which embraced
a culture of permissiveness that was shocking to most of their parents.
Not only did many of these students openly drink, smoke, do drugs,
and engage in premarital sex, they also grew their hair out and listened
to rock music. Their social values were in stark contrast to their parent's
generation, too. Concepts such as women's liberation, racial equality,
and environmentalism, while by no means new ideas, had never been
embraced by previous generations as enthusiastically as they were by the
boomers. Terrell, then, was often placed directly in the middle between
the counterculture and the "silent majority," and both groups were large
and extremely influential. Balancing the needs and wants of both groups
was essentially impossible and Terrell's efforts to find solutions equitable
to both sides often satisfied neither. As a result, he attracted numerous
critics on both sides.

Those who disagreed with Terrell did so with remarkable venom,
bordering on abject hatred, and much of that anger remains today among
his biggest detractors. Among those faculty and alumni who are critical
of Terrell, the chief complaints are that he was a weak and ineffectual
leader who gave in too easily to student demands. A number of faculty
also felt that Terrell did little to support them and frequently refused to
listen to their concerns. Some also felt that he was too friendly with the
regents. "I don't think I have ever seen a person who was better at the
care and feeding of Regents," quipped Raymond Muse, who chaired
the history department during the beginning of Terrell's presidency.
Muse even confessed that it was his "disillusionment" with Terrell that
convinced him to retire early. Muse conceded that he thought Terrell
a man of good intentions, but stated "I think he was in many ways a

A photo staged and taken by student Brian A. Sims of the WSU Cinema Guild in 1976 as part of a fund-raising drive, and as a parody of Grant Wood's *American Gothic. Historic WSU Photographs Collection, pc004b35bfterrfam_1976pullmangothic. WSU MASC.*

disaster for the university." Another retired professor of English at WSU, Paul Brians, further elaborated in a 2018 interview on the concern that Terrell did not listen to faculty:

> Terrell was always very proud of telling people his door was always open—that he would talk to anybody. To a limited degree that was true. . . . You couldn't change his mind. He rarely gave in to anything that came at him from an opposing direction. . . . He had this

condescending manner in which he would sort of try to calmly soothe you and calm you down . . . he would give these speeches that were just agony. They were just awful to listen to when he was speaking so simplistically, and we [the faculty senate] all thought that he was a dim bulb, he didn't understand the intellectual life, didn't understand student life, didn't understand the activism around him at all.

While Terrell was raked over the coals during his presidency, time has proved far kinder to his legacy. Terrell is widely remembered by former WSU employees and alumni as the "Student's President." Though it is difficult to determine who first came up with this term, or when it was first used, it is one of the most common titles ascribed to Terrell. Almost all who remember him fondly bring up his relationship with students. "He was here for the students; WSU strengthened itself in its character under his leadership. There was a lot to be done in learning the very basics in working together as a diverse population, and he was just the man to do that," mused Sue Hinz ('70) in a 2018 interview. "There is no one who could have got the university through those unrest years any better than he did," said Terrell's secretary, Gen DeVleming in a 1986 interview. "We'd have forty or fifty irate kids come storming into the office . . . if Dr. Terrell was there, his tall, lean, lanky frame, he'd come strolling out of his office and of course everyone would shut up when they saw him and he'd say 'do we have a problem?' and he'd take them all in the Regents Room . . . and he'd have them in there for an hour and I just couldn't believe it. Then within an hour's time, they'd start coming out in twos and threes, quietly talking about what they'd been discussing." Student activists from Terrell's presidency also recalled him fondly, even those who found themselves in opposition to him. "I [do] think he set a wonderful standard in his interactions with students . . . it was empowering for me as a student to be able to talk to the person in charge," remarked Karen Troianello ('80) (née Karen Blair, the lead plaintiff in the *Blair* case). "He was open to learning about the views others held and he saw the value of reaching a compromise to the betterment of the University and all of its constituents," wrote Nola Cross

('70), who chaired the Ad Hoc Committee Against Racism during the student strike. "He [later] provided an excellent letter of reference for me." The fact that Terrell would listen so widely to student concerns, and personally lend generous support to students who opposed him, was something of a unique trait for a university president. His readiness to acknowledge that systemic issues existed within the university and his willingness to discuss those issues with students ultimately won him the admiration of much of the student body.

In addition to making a point to talk to students, Terrell was a frequent ally of student-friendly initiatives. Terrell supported the expansion of the student newspaper, the *Evergreen*, from publishing three days a week to five days a week. When students clamored for the preservation of the historic Stevens and Stimson dormitories, Terrell added his weight to that measure as well. When a female student came to Terrell asking for the university to implement co-ed dormitories at WSU, he recalls inviting her to speak in front of the regents to argue her case. WSU announced the integration of the first co-ed dorms in March of 1970. He also supported the establishment of the student-run KZUU, a third university radio station which supplemented the already long established KWSU and KUGR. In the fall of 1971, Terrell announced a university directive wherein the university would cede one of its FM frequencies to KUGR, granting it a permanent home on the FM waves. (KUGR would give up its FM frequency for an internet format in the early 21st century.) Terrell himself made good use of the public airwaves—in the early '80s he delivered a weekly radio address on KWSU. Terrell's speeches, usually five minutes or less, covered a variety of topics, including the importance of public history as an emerging field of study, the necessity of curbing NCAA athletic recruiting violations, university convocation, and in one address he personally exhorted the university to support and sustain its performing arts program in order to contribute to the culture and vibrancy of the WSU community.

Throughout the controversy and unrest which roiled WSU during Terrell's presidency, Terrell maintained a steady hand and calm demeanor.

His ability to weather the storms of the '60s and '70s allowed for the university to prosper and grow, and set up his successor, Sam Smith, to take WSU to even greater heights. Few individuals would be capable of doing as much. It was no simple task—one requiring patience, grace, and resolve. Even his staunchest critics conceded that Terrell's patience was legendary. The man was unflappable. When Pullman was beset by protest, Terrell committed to resolving the crisis peacefully. While some see this as a sign of weakness, it can also be viewed as a sign of strength. Terrell could have taken the easy way out and called in the police and National Guard to break up the protests—as seen on other campuses during this time—but he did not. He resolved to let the voices of the students, faculty, and alumni of Washington State University on all sides be heard. Most importantly, he listened.

RESEARCH NOTES

The majority of the research done for this chapter was conducted in the Manuscripts, Archives, and Special Collections of the WSU Libraries. Collections used include the Office of the President: W. Glenn Terrell Inauguration Records and Photographs (UA 162); the President's Office Records 1953–1985 (Archives 207); the Harold Romberg Protest Papers 1970 (Archives 278); and Office of the President: Glenn Terrell Records 1967–1976 (Archives 205).

Sue Hinz, Paul Brians, and the late Jim Short graciously granted interviews about the Terrell years. Karen Troianello (née Blair) and Nola Cross also provided insight for the project via email correspondence.

Oral histories conducted as part of the WSU Centennial Project were greatly beneficial to my research—they are freely available on the WSU Libraries Digital Collections website. Interviews drawn upon include those given by Richard Fry, David Stratton, Edward Bennett, Raymond Muse, Wallis Beasley, Richard Hume, Gen DeVleming, and Glenn Terrell. The WSU centennial volumes written by Richard Fry, George Frykman, and William Stimson provided important background information.

Terrell in his office, 1985.
Historic WSU
Photographs Collection,
c004b35bfTerrelport_1985office2.
WSU MASC.

Also of help were scanned issues of WSU's former alumni magazine, *Hilltopics*, as well scanned issues of the *Evergreen* (now called the *Daily Evergreen*). Marc Arsell Robinson's 2012 dissertation on the black student movement at WSU also provided important information, particularly in regard to the AGR case. All of the above are available online through the WSU Libraries.

Thank you to Jennifer Laine at the Washington State Law Library and Brenda Cloninger at the Whitman County Courthouse for tracking down the legal documentation surrounding *Blair v. Washington State University*. The legal citation for the case is 108 Wn.2d 558.

Special thanks to Kenton Bird, Pat Caraher, Sue Hinz, David Stratton, Michael Short, Trevor Bond, and Mark O'English for providing leads on this project. Finally, thanks to Brian Stack, Nancy Lust, and Lee Ann Powell for editing the manuscript of this chapter.

Samuel H. Smith
1985–2000

BY BRIAN STACK

*A*S A CHILD SAMUEL H. SMITH SEEMED AN unlikely candidate for a university presidency. Born on February 4, 1940, Smith was raised in a single-parent family on welfare in the rural farming area of Salinas, California, a region still reeling from the troubles of the Great Depression. Smith worked in the lettuce fields to help his mother, a medical secretary, after losing his father in an accident at age five. Smith met his future wife, Pat, at the local high school. Sam tested well in school, yet many at the time doubted whether someone raised among poor migrant farm workers could succeed in higher education. Smith believed his upbringing made him more likely to end up in jail than in college. But even at a young age he showed an uncanny ability to convince others to give him opportunities to show what he could do. And so, when the University of California, Berkeley decided to reach out to students whose backgrounds made opportunities for higher education rare, Smith seized on the new initiative. His excellence in education, and industrious work ethic cultivated through toil alongside migrant farm workers, made Smith a logical recipient of one of the six scholarships that Berkeley created to target these young people. More than fifty years of service to higher education followed.

165

Smith excelled at Berkeley as an undergraduate and earned a bachelor's degree in plant pathology in 1961, not long after marrying his high school sweetheart. Because of his excellence as an undergraduate he was invited into Berkeley's doctoral program, earning a doctorate in plant pathology in 1964. By age 24 the department had offered him a position on their faculty. Smith's impeccable research credentials—including work as a NATO postdoctoral fellow in England—brought him to the attention of Pennsylvania State University, which offered him a faculty position in plant pathology. From there, Smith moved up the ranks of university administration while publishing over 100 articles. When dean of the College of Agriculture, he and Pat crisscrossed Pennsylvania's sixty-seven counties seeking support for university projects. In each county he gave a similar speech that implored legislators and community leaders to invest in the state institution or welcome a Penn State branch campus.

By 1985 Smith's successful fundraising and institutional development made him an outstanding presidential candidate to address challenges facing Washington State University. Smith was in fact such a good fit for the university presidency that he did not even need to apply. He discovered that he had been nominated for the position when his mentors called to let him know that he was now one of three finalists for succeeding Glenn Terrell. After Smith visited the campus and met with various university officials, the WSU Board of Regents offered him the job.

Coming from Penn State, Smith had much to learn about WSU's culture and history. To rectify this, Smith began calling on previous presidents. He and Pat visited former President C. Clement French at his home and spoke at length about life as university president. Back in Pullman, Smith befriended the daughter of former President Enoch Bryan, Gertrude Bryan Gannon, who helped acquaint Smith with important local people the best way she knew—touring the local cemetery. While they walked the quiet grounds together she would use the gravestones to teach Smith about the people who had shaped the institution's history. These walks helped educate Smith about the history of the university he was about to lead.

Sam Smith converses with his predecessor, Glenn Terrell.
Historic WSU Photographs Collection, pc004b35bf1. WSU MASC.

At the same time, Smith needed to set his own goals for his term. At the advice of Clark Kerr, chancellor and future president of the University of California system, and John W. Oswald, future president of Penn State and the University of Kentucky, Smith developed a "4–1" approach. He identified four goals that could be measured quantitatively and one goal that could be measured qualitatively. The four quantitative goals were to expand the university into three branch campuses, to graduate one third of the total graduates in WSU's history, to increase by tenfold the number of research grants, and to raise significant private funds for the university. The qualitative goal was to increase equity at WSU.

WHEN SMITH CAME TO THE UNIVERSITY TO BEGIN HIS
fifteen years of service, he brought a different leadership style. He contrasted himself with predecessor Glenn Terrell by saying that he was
less likely to walk up to someone, shake their hand, and say "Hi, I'm
Sam Smith," than he was to wander into a building on campus late
at night, find the room where the light was still on, and ask a faculty
member about their research. As such, Smith was just as likely to know
the name of a nightly custodian as faculty. He also had the skills of a
master politician and artful fundraiser. He possessed the rare ability
to persuade a room full of business leaders or legislators to come out
in support of an initiative. Smith bargained, negotiated, and compromised with anyone who would talk to him in order to secure funding
and support for university projects. During his tenure the university
expanded its geographical reach to include three additional campuses.
Almost 40 percent of graduates to that point in the university's history
were educated during Smith's tenure. WSU's faculty grew in prestige
as almost $760 million in capital improvements and over $275 million
in other fundraising was accomplished. It was during this era that the
university first had faculty elected to the National Academy of Science. Smith was an excellent fundraiser and die-hard advocate for state
and private investment in university education. His leadership abilities
combined able fundraising with the ability to bring people together to
focus on cooperation and compromise. In so doing, he helped increase
the university's presence and stature in the state and around the world.

The biggest challenge Smith had to address as president, and what
occupied most of his time at the institution, was the opening of three
"branch campuses" around the state, today part of the six-campus WSU
system. These campuses were designed to increase WSU's presence
beyond Pullman and increase focus on specific issues facing Washington state. To make this happen Smith not only built upon the work of
previous WSU presidents, but also took the university in a bold new
direction. In 1989 the Washington state legislature formalized a process
already launched before Smith arrived by officially designating three

WSU branch campuses in Spokane, the Tri-Cities, and Vancouver. These three campuses have been successful since their inception, but that success was not always assured. Expanding the campus system involved a mixture of local politics, fundraising, educational challenges, and technological innovation. Accomplishing the task required the leadership of a university president skilled in negotiation and persistent enough to see those changes through.

Each of the campuses required a unique response to a similar set of issues, so it is helpful to understand the challenges facing branch campus expansion by looking at some of the broader problems in higher education in Washington state during the late 1980s and 1990s. The university "turf wars," a term disliked by President Smith but used widely during that time, were public disputes between Washington state's three public universities that were most impacted by the new campuses: WSU, the University of Washington (UW), and Eastern Washington University (EWU). The disputes focused primarily on the regions of the state in which each would operate, and how each would administer education. Smith found himself navigating the rival interests of university presidents, state legislators, and city councils during these "turf wars."

UW argued that its Seattle location meant it should be the go-to university for education on the west side of the state. EWU in Cheney, a small town about fifteen miles southwest of Spokane, was trying to reformulate itself from a regional college into a research institution. Officials feared offering WSU free rein in Spokane, the biggest city on the "east side," might relegate EWU to relative obscurity.

The WSU–UW relationship over expansion had a rocky start, but it did not take long for Smith and UW President William Gerberding to realize that far more could be accomplished by working together. This may have upset some Cougar football fans, who saw their team lose eleven of the fifteen cross-state Apple Cup games against UW during Smith's tenure. But off the gridiron, cooperation made more sense than rivalry. Getting UW on board, however, required some heavy lifting. At the time UW was not enthusiastic about branch campuses for fear of funding being diverted from its main campus. Smith, on the other hand, believed UW support for branch campuses was crucial for advocating to state legislators. Smith sensed that UW would not balk at sharing in the benefits of an expanded presence throughout the state, and cleverly developed a plan to garner support.

Smith traveled to Tacoma and met with local officials who hoped to attract one of the state's universities to establish a satellite campus in their city. WSU's previous investment in a Vancouver campus made expanding so quickly to another city on the west side of the state unlikely, but that did not mean this was not an opportunity. Smith hired a helicopter to fly around Tacoma under the guise of scouting locations for a new campus (knowing full-well that one does not select the location for a campus based on a bird's-eye view). After the attention-grabbing air tour with local civic leaders, Smith returned to Pullman, saying that if the city did not hear back from UW in a week, WSU would put in an offer for a location in Tacoma. Within 48 hours of the helicopter tour UW expressed their support for opening a branch campus in the city. From then on, WSU and UW cooperated when lobbying state legislators about the need to dedicate funds for the selection and opening of branch campuses. Smith's leadership on this issue was recognized during his retirement ceremony when a photo of him giving a plaque to UW, designating it as a WSU branch campus, caused some light-hearted commotion.

Earning the trust of Eastern Washington University was a very different battle. EWU, like universities throughout Washington during the mid-1980s, was going through financial struggles. EWU claimed that its status as the public provider of higher education closest to Spokane made it the obvious selection for a campus in the city. But Smith also recognized the potential of a Spokane branch campus for the prestige and impact of WSU. Thus, Smith and others at the university appealed to Washington state's Higher Education Coordinating Board (HECB) for the right to educate alongside EWU in Spokane. This sparked some fears among members of the EWU administration and Board of Trustees about whether the university would simply be absorbed into WSU altogether. Even after the HECB agreed to a higher education master plan in March 1987 that allowed both universities to educate in Spokane, some still feared a merger. The universities instead found ways to share education and research responsibilities: WSU would offer courses and majors that EWU was unable to provide. Fears about mergers, educational responsibilities, and shared governance seem, in retrospect, overblown. The university "turf wars," fueled by statewide budget constraints, quickly fizzled out. Compromise and cooperation were important aspects of Smith's leadership approach. When traveling around Washington state to meet with regents, trustees, legislators, or other university presidents Smith listened, bargained, and negotiated, but stood firm on his core principle—to establish WSU's ability to educate throughout the state.

The university's expansion to the Tri-Cities reflected the benefits of this cooperative approach. That campus was officially placed in January 1989 at the Tri-Cities University Center (TUC) in Richland. Legislators from each of the three cities (Richland, Pasco, and Kennewick) agreed to compromise on a location for a branch campus so long as academic issues guided the decision-making process. The major disagreement was over whether to hold graduate studies in the TUC building in Richland and upper-division undergraduate education at Columbia Basin Community College (CBCC) in Pasco—or to locate all programs on one campus. Smith decided that locating all activities in one place and in one city—the TUC in Richland—would make recruiting faculty, commuting, and earning accreditation easier. He recognized, moreover, that the university would not abandon CBCC just because the branch campus was located in Richland. Because WSU Tri-Cities then only provided upper-division and graduate-level courses, CBCC was still needed to provide lower-division courses. Thus, cooperation with CBCC was crucial to transfer students' success at WSU Tri-Cities.

WSU's expansion to Vancouver had started before Smith's arrival at WSU, but WSU did not have an official campus, instead relying on Clark College for class space. Like elsewhere, Smith skillfully balanced the interests of HECB, WSU, and local community members overseeing

Smith and others at the dedication of the Vancouver campus,
June 28, 1996. From left, Joe Clark, president Clark Community
College; Sen. Al Bauer; Rep. Don Carlson; Mr. and Sen. Val Ogden;
Governor Mike Lowry; Hal Dengerink, dean of WSU Vancouver;
Pete Pickett, president Lower Columbia Community College; and
President Smith. *President Sam Smith Memorabilia, ua2000-14b2f3.
WSU MASC.*

the project to secure a location for a new campus in 1990, settling on the
Salmon Creek site. On May 13 the Vancouver campus held its first local
commencement, awarding degrees to 38 graduates. Construction was
soon underway and WSU Vancouver moved into its own 348-acre campus for the 1996–1997 academic year. A year later the campus expanded
even further with construction of a $16 million engineering and life
sciences building and a $9 million multimedia classroom building fin-
ishing soon after Smith's retirement.

When it came to actually constructing a Spokane campus, Smith again deployed his typical leadership style. He drew on his past experiences working with other public institutions such as the University of California, Berkeley, whose model provided some inspiration for WSU branch campus development. This incorporated his belief that one must learn university histories in order to lead effectively. Additionally, Smith tried to downplay conflicts that arose from local politics. In 1988 Smith brought in Robert Scannell from Penn State to help guide the selection process in Spokane. As an outside consultant—but one that Smith trusted—Scannell's presence helped remove some of the friction that arose from WSU–EWU merger discussions. Scannell recommended WSU expand to the Riverfront area of Spokane across the Spokane River from Gonzaga University. The HECB and state legislators quickly agreed to the proposal, but it took some cajoling from Smith to ensure a more than $800,000 appropriation was put it into action. Together with other institutions of higher education in Spokane, WSU began building a new research facility. Over time, the Spokane campus has earned a reputation as a respected center for medical research and innovation enhanced by new facilities, technologies, and programs. The campus also hosted conferences on major health problems like the AIDS crisis, which caused so much public devastation in the late 1980s and early 1990s. Such activities helped solidify the importance of the Spokane branch campus to both WSU and the state at large.

The Tri-Cities campus experienced similar developments. In 1991 WSU completed a $12.1 million building, tripling the size of its temporary location in the Tri-Cities University Building. The new building included a library to help solidify the educational presence of the branch campus. Later projects included expansions related to the Hanford nuclear site, the environment, and agricultural issues. Because it was located next to Richland High School—a fact on Smith's mind when selecting the location—the branch campus was well-integrated into the community and provided local students with an obvious place to transfer after completing lower-division courses at community colleges. In 2007 the Tri-Cities campus opened to freshman and sophomore students and currently it operates as a four-year university with a graduate school. And so, it is no surprise that Smith's politicking, fundraising, and hard work earned him the designation of father of the branch campuses in Washington state.

Despite Smith's adept political skills, a truce in the "turf wars" was not enough to get these campuses built. Significant funding, both private and public, was essential. During Smith's presidency, the university underwent a significant fiscal transformation with private money becoming an essential component of public university budgets. When he took office, the university faced serious budget constraints and financial controversies. Some of these had roots preceding Smith's arrival, such as legislators' massive cut to the university budget and a controversy over presidential pay. But many new challenges arose during Smith's tenure. In order to build three different campuses, and make much needed improvements to facilities and new construction in Pullman, Smith had to navigate a tricky political climate. State legislators sometimes proposed cutbacks to funds essential to running the university's day-to-day activities, but increased support for capital projects allowing the university to build, expand, and grow. Smith's job during this precarious financial climate was not only to convince state legislators to open public coffers when they were reluctant to do so, but to encourage private donors to open their checkbooks. In doing so, Smith helped the university shatter its own private donation records and convince legislators to support even-greater appropriations.

ONE OF SMITH'S FOUR QUANTITATIVE GOALS WAS increasing the number of research grants at WSU. He long believed department budgetary funding should not be a faculty member's only research support, but at the time this was somewhat controversial. Smith recalled one experience while working as a faculty member as Penn State.

He was summoned to his department chair's office after earning a large grant. His chair scolded him for taking grant money because it would give the perception that his own department was not providing adequate support for his research. Smith, of course, still took the money. Such a story is indicative of Smith's approach for getting funds for faculty research—look everywhere. Outside investment in faculty research, whether from national grants or private donors, would soon become a staple of university instruction. Smith sought out donors to help improve the quality of technology on campus, encouraged the university faculty to look for impressive grant proposals, and consistently lobbied the state for additional education funds. His approach is perhaps best summed up in a talk he gave in 1987 at the WSU Alumni Leaders Conference: "I'll support any scheme to add funds for higher education except highway robbery, although highway robbery could be discussed."

This take-any-measure approach to gaining funds for the university achieved big successes. Smith relished people joking that they needed to keep a close eye on their wallets whenever they were in the same room as him. Smith had an astonishing ability to talk someone into becoming a first-time donor, or, if they had donated before, to give even more. As such, he initiated the university's first comprehensive fundraising effort, Campaign WSU, which raised $275.4 million, despite a goal of "only" $250 million. Such a massive influx of money was essential to funding WSU's expansion in Pullman and at the branch campuses. In Pullman, the veterinary medicine program constructed a $22.7 million building for research on animal disease and biotechnology, as well as a $38 million veterinary teaching hospital.

Such grants were not just limited to the sciences. In 1987 President Smith and the director of the Washington State University Museum of Art were happy to see the formation of a new endowment, Friends of the Museum of Art, which set out to raise $20,000 for the museum in its first year and $500,000 over a decade. Although trained as a scientist, Smith long recognized the need for investment in the arts and humanities; his wife, Pat, was also dedicated to the arts and supported the creation of the Glenn Terrell Friendship Mall. Additionally, state and private money came together to facilitate the construction of numerous projects in Pullman: the Bookie campus bookstore was redone; the Holland Library expanded with a new wing, which eventually became the Glenn Terrell Library; a new Recreation Center was built; and many other buildings were constructed, torn down, or modernized as the campus underwent cosmetic renovation. And this was all separate from the millions of dollars that went into building the branch campuses. Smith led the way on this expansion by using his friendly personality and connections with legislators, business executives, and alumni to encourage donations to the university. More than ever before, Smith built up the expectation that graduates should give back to their alma mater—and there was a never-ending series of projects to which they could contribute.

Part of Smith's job as president was to lobby the state for money on behalf of the university; WSU was still a land-grant, publicly funded institution. Unfortunately, according to Washington's HECB, state spending on higher education was ranked 46th in the country in 1986. Such dismal funding numbers made it no surprise that the state was also in the bottom half nationally for the number of graduate degrees offered. With WSU and UW now both devoted to expanding branch campuses, funding concerns seemed ever more likely to be a source of conflict. But instead, WSU and UW worked together when submitting funding proposals to the state, especially during 1989 when the funding and construction of the branch campuses was in full swing. At the advice of the governor, yet also characteristic of the way Smith approached possible funding conflicts between the universities, WSU and UW secured $45 million in funding for expanding branch campuses from the state for the 1990–1991 fiscal year. That this $45 million was going into a general fund for expansion upset some legislators who worried whether the funds would be equitably distributed, but the pooled money reflected the university's approach of cooperation with other institutions of higher education.

One of the most important projects for which Smith helped secure state funding was improvement of the Washington Higher Education

Sam and Pat Smith, 1986. *Historic WSU Photographs Collection, pc004b35c. WSU MASC.*

Telecommunications System (WHETS). In order for the university to provide affordable education at branch campuses, it needed technology that allowed faculty to instruct without actually traveling large distances to be in each classroom for every session. Long before the internet made online and distance learning a staple of modern higher education, Washington State University was developing technologies to do just that. The solution was WHETS. The system equipped classrooms on the Pullman and branch campuses with cameras, televisions, and audio/ visual equipment that allowed an instructor to teach a typical class while transmitting to televisions in classrooms across the state. Both students and faculty were able to interact with one another during these classes. Exams were proctored locally, while essays and other written materials, such as feedback on those assignments, were sent via 24-hour courier. In the later years of Smith's presidency, the internet would further expand this ability.

The first WHETS classes were offered on branch campuses in 1985 and expanded quickly to include the University of Idaho, Gonzaga University, and UW within its first few years. In 1990 Smith helped secure almost $3 million to expand WHETS, a major victory indicative of the investments in technology which defined his presidency. By 1998 there were 32 multimedia classrooms connected to the WHETS system, including six on the Pullman campus. Once the branch campuses were more firmly established, WHETS did more than just relay classes; it hosted meetings between faculty and students on various campuses and broadcast some open forums with WSU administrators. Smith realized that technological innovations like WHETS were going to be the new frontiers of higher education and pressed for deep investments in them.

Private firms also made technological investments at WSU. Apple Inc.'s donation of 21 computers—which received better publicity than Paul Allen's generous donation upgrading a fraternity with new technology—helped both faculty and students access relevant information and use the latest educational techniques. Infrastructure improvements from AT&T and WSU's connection to Internet2—a multi-university information system—further solidified WSU as a premier provider of technology-based higher education. In 1992 WSU received its largest-ever single corporate donation to that point: $5.5 million in software from Mentor Graphics Corporation.

Students attending WSU during the 2010s expect their lectures will make use of computer software like PowerPoint to deliver content. Until the early 1990s, however, most universities, WSU included, did not have the technology to provide such lectures. WSU's technological advancements between 1985 and 2000 were awarded various prizes and featured in multiple *New York Times* articles discussing revolutions in higher education. Overhead projectors and chalkboards did not disappear from the university during Smith's time in office, but he helped initiate a breadth of technological changes on the Pullman and branch campuses that would increasingly render those tools obsolete. Smith's successes with digital education led him to be asked to become a founding member of Western Governors University, an online university based in Utah offering education and distance learning to thousands of individuals annually.

Despite the successes of various funding drives, and the many frequent-flyer miles that Smith earned traversing the state, fundraising could not always make up for the deficit caused by state budget woes and increased university spending. Even when state legislators offered modest increases in state funding, they rarely matched the rate at which the cost of education was growing. As a result, the rising cost of education was increasingly met by rising student tuition and fees. According to the WSU Budget Office, for the 1985–1986 school year rounded in-state tuition rates were $1,600 for undergraduates and $2,300 for graduate students. When Smith left during the 1999–2000 school year, in-state tuition and fees had risen to $3,500 for undergraduates and $5,500 for graduate students. Nonresident tuition and fee rates increased from $4,500 for undergraduates and $5,800 for graduate students in 1985–1986 to $10,600 for undergraduates and $13,400 for graduate students for the 1999–2000 academic year. Veterinary medicine students faced similar trends.

Increasing education costs were always a source of consternation for students, but this soon became the new standard for university fiscal policy. Until the 1986–1987 school year, state law limited tuition and fees increases to every two years. Inevitably, rates often jumped significantly after a year of holding steady. Beginning in 1987, however, a legislative reversal allowed tuition rates to increase gradually on an annual basis. During Smith's time in office, tuition and fees increased by 10 percent or more three times, but most often by just under 4 percent. This trend increased even more dramatically after Smith retired.

From year to year, tuition increases threatened to decrease enrollment, but overall enrollment blossomed during Smith's tenure. By 2000 just under 40 percent of all WSU graduates had attended WSU while Smith was president. The expansion of branch campuses helped spur along graduation rates, but WSU also made sure to offer funding opportunities for those who could not meet the rising costs of education. The Glenn Terrell Presidential Scholars program, whose first awardees attended WSU the year following President Terrell's retirement, is one example of such new scholarship opportunities. Smith secured millions of dollars in additional private and state donations to create other scholarship funds. Creating an affordable education was part of the branch campus mandate. Students on branch campuses could take night classes while working jobs, parenting, or both, thus defraying the costs associated with moving to and living in Pullman.

EXPANDING THE UNIVERSITY ADDRESSED MANY OF Smith's "4–1" goals, but he also recognized the need to focus on problems in Pullman. Those who most criticized Smith during his presidency complained that his politicking and fundraising often resulted in him being absent from the Pullman campus. Yet Smith did make an effort to address issues on the main campus. Every year Sam and Pat welcomed around 2,000 guests to the president's house, whose central location led the Smiths to dub it "the brick fish bowl." They heard directly from students and faculty about the kind of changes they wanted WSU to make. Some of these changes were addressed through fundraising efforts, but other changes needed to be made that impacted student life. During his tenure WSU reformed its course requirements and alcohol policies while working to create an equitable campus for minority students, faculty, and staff.

A major change to university curriculum was the introduction of "core" course requirements. If WSU was going to ensure students could lead once they graduated, then students needed standardized classes that prepared them with basic skills. Besides ensuring that students were better educated, the curricula reforms were related to the qualitative goal in Smith's 4–1 approach: facilitating an equitable and diverse campus. The

President Smith traveled to Nihon University as part of WSU's global efforts. Here he takes part in a ceremonial sake barrel opening, 1989. *President Sam Smith Memorabilia, ua2000-14b1. WSU MASC.*

curricula reform committee brought to campus leading scholars in Asian studies and world history, such as the famed historian Peter Stearns, to educate WSU faculty on new issues and develop curricula for core courses. The new standards created two required world civilizations courses.

These world civilizations courses—consciously avoiding the "Western" label—recognized that an increasingly globalized world meant the university needed to look to the Pacific, not just to Europe. Thus, students had to be engaged with issues important to China and Japan, as well as other parts of Asia and the world, such as Africa. This focus allowed faculty to bring in more women's and minority perspectives, increasing the cultural competency of WSU graduates. Students were becoming increasingly better equipped to take on the challenges of the globalizing world in the late 1980s and 1990s. Smith's trip to Nihon University in Japan, where he was awarded an honorary doctorate, is one measure of success on that front. He also received an honorary doctorate from the Far Eastern State University in Vladivostok, Russia, in recognition of WSU's considerable assistance. Newly developed student exchange programs with Japan and Russia—and even a brief consideration of opening a branch campus in Japan—spoke to the worldwide prestige WSU was building under Smith and the connections his gregarious personality helped develop.

The world civilizations courses also coordinated readings with the English department, which itself made changes to the English 101 course on composition. Students now were introduced consistently to the classical texts of Western civilization, but also to more diverse perspectives. President Smith advocated, especially, for the importance of writing to this new education standard. Some in the more traditional sciences and engineering fields were skeptical of the need for "writing across the curriculum," but many soon came around. President Smith recalled meeting a group of students that had visited Boeing to speak to the company's CEO about the kinds of skills expected of them when coming out of WSU. After the visit, the students returned to campus somewhat surprised—but supporting the new writing standards—when they learned that Boeing wanted workers who would be able to write clear and concise technical reports in addition to the basic skills they developed in their major classes. In 1993 Boeing made a donation of $7 million over two years, bringing their total contribution to $8.6 million. This closeness between private industry, university education, and student employment resulted in WSU being ranked 34th nationally in corporate financial support in 1991. Not only was Smith early to this kind of fiscal development, he was good at it.

These changes helped set up WSU students to take the lead on global issues following graduation. Students were introduced to computer usage and how to access a library database, skills we perhaps now take for granted with our tendency to "Google" any question. As with the expansion of the university to new campuses, Smith recognized new technologies were essential to introducing a new set of education standards and best practices for the rest of the country. And while we now see the obvious need to look at issues with a global perspective, that was not always such a truism. Most of the WSU students who graduated during Smith's tenure were facing a very different global world than their predecessors. The end of the Cold War and the dismantling of the Berlin Wall brought about a new global power structure. The United States emerged as the seemingly single global superpower. The answer to the question of how to navigate the world and the issues of the 1990s, 2000s, and beyond, would—for these students—be grounded in their educational experiences at WSU.

While the changes to the curricula created happy students, the reforms to the university alcohol policy led to some unhappy ones. But in order to graduate more students, increase faculty support, be awarded significant research grants, and increase equity and diversity on campus, Smith had to implement changes to help reform WSU's reputation. When Congress passed the National Minimum Drinking Age Act in 1984, essentially forcing each state to increase its drinking age to 21, underage WSU students were no longer allowed to drink legally in Moscow, Idaho, before returning across the state border to Pullman. Additionally, the goal of removing Pullman's reputation as a party campus required the university to focus on issues stemming from alcohol. In 1998 Smith called on the Greek system to pass a new policy and banned open drinking in fraternities, although members could still drink in their rooms if of legal age. Smith hoped a Greek-initiated policy change would be more effective than a simple executive decision.

Unfortunately, not all students embraced these changes. In May 1998 WSU police responded to an incident near a fraternity keg party and soon found themselves under attack from party goers. By 2:00 a.m., 93 officers, including 46 from Idaho, were attempting to control a growing riot of hundreds of students chanting in protest of the new alcohol policy. Five hours after the entire event began, the ruckus was over, but 23 officers were injured, three people were arrested, and around $15,000 worth of property had been damaged. As a result, three fraternities received sanctions and nineteen people were convicted for crimes relating to the incident. Although it is indeed quite difficult to downplay the significance of a small-scale student riot, Smith tried to find a way to not demonize WSU students at large; most had not participated in the rioting. Perhaps because the riot quite clearly demonstrated the need for a new approach to drinking and partying on campus, changes to the alcohol policy stood. In 2001 the commitment to the new policies resulted in the *Princeton Review* removing WSU from its Top 20 list of party schools.

Smith also turned his attention to issues of equity. In 1987, the Washington State Supreme Court ruled in *Blair v. Washington State University* that the Title IX mandate requiring equal spending on men's and women's sports did not allow an exemption for football spending. As a result, WSU needed to spend significantly more money on women's athletics to bring itself into compliance with the law despite having already done so as a result of lower court decisions in the *Blair* case during Terrell's presidency. Smith, as both a public supporter of the WSU football program and a longstanding advocate for women's equality, was forced to make difficult decisions about which men's athletic programs to cut in order to provide more funding for women's athletics. Some students complained about the cuts to rifling and wrestling that came from the *Blair* decision, but Smith stood steady on making these changes, despite their unpopularity to some. The changes to the student alcohol policy or the cuts to well-liked sports programs surely were going to upset some students, but these were important changes to make for a modern, respected, equitable university.

The student body of the new university looked quite different at the end of Smith's presidency than at the beginning. Smith was dedicated to diversity on campus. He hired recruitment officers, created minority student services, devoted money to programs focused on diversifying

Kappa Kappa Gamma presents Smith with an award on Sam and Pat Smith Day, April 17, 2000. *President Sam Smith Memorabilia, ua2000-14b1. WSU MASC.*

the racial homogeneity of the WSU student body and even marched with minority students to protest inequality. During his time, WSU opened its first multicultural and LGBTA centers to help institutionalize WSU's support for minority issues. As a result, the percentage of minority students increased from 7 percent at the beginning of his tenure to 13 percent in 1999. This near doubling of the percentage of minority students helps give context to Smith's hope for creating a multicultural student body. It may not have been the radical demographic change that some students hoped to see, but WSU was now more in line with the population of Washington state generally, which, according to the 2000 census had a non-white or mixed-race population of just over 18 percent.

Smith was also committed to minority faculty recruitment and retention, a longtime and continuing struggle for the rural Pullman campus. When Smith arrived, faculty salaries at WSU, for minority and non-minority faculty alike, lagged behind their peers at other comparable institutions. However, Smith took his typical approach of studying an

Smith in front of the Center for Undergraduate Education
that bears his name. *Washington State Magazine archives.*

issue and making compromises to institute a step-pay system and pay-equity studies and reforms, and find state funding to help bring the salaries of WSU faculty more in line with their peers. This, of course, did not solve every problem relating to recruiting and retaining faculty while making sure that men and women, white and nonwhite, were all paid equally and felt welcome at the institution. But Smith engaged university faculty, staff, and students to ensure that WSU was a more diverse institution when he left office than when he took the helm.

Part of Smith's success in diversifying WSU came from his belief that diversity did not just apply to the racial makeup of the classroom. By expanding the branch campuses to areas underserved by major universities, many older, non-traditional students in Spokane, Tri-Cities, and Vancouver—as well as place-bound students in cities without campuses once the internet and distance learning programs had developed more fully—were able to receive an education they might otherwise have missed if they had to reside on or near the Pullman campus. Students in Pullman who took WHETS classes benefited from the perspectives of a different class culture where the professor was now not the only person over age 30 in the room. Smith's dedication to scholarships offsetting the growing cost of education helped erase some of the class-related barriers that had prevented people from attending WSU. Although best known for his work with branch campuses, Smith listened, negotiated, and compromised to help improve the Pullman campus, from the quality of the education to its international reputation and the diversity of the WSU community.

Due to his leadership on equity issues, the Association for Faculty Women created the Sam H. Smith Leadership Award in 2000. But such recognition of Smith's work was not confined to WSU. After bringing athletics back from funding struggles, Smith was elected as chair of the NCAA Executive Committee in 1997. He also served on the Kellogg Commission on the Future of State and Land-Grant Universities, and was chair of Presidents and Chancellors of the Pacific-10 in 1993 and 1994, as well as chair of the Washington State Council of Presidents for 1990–1991 and 1996–1997. These are only some of the numerous regional and national boards on which he served, four of which he created himself. In short, his successful leadership on many issues facing higher education meant that numerous organizations wanted him on their boards and chairing their committees.

THOSE FAMILIAR WITH SMITH'S WORK ETHIC WERE NOT surprised that although he left the university's presidency in 2000, he did not leave the university. Instead, he and Pat, herself a dedicated fighter in the battles that Smith continually waged, moved to Seattle where he still occupies an office in a WSU building. Smith continues to raise significant money for the university every year. In 2002 the $40 million Center for Undergraduate Education (the CUE) opened, and, quite fittingly given his contribution to building at the university, the center was dedicated to President Smith. In 2016 the WSU Foundation awarded him the Weldon B. Gibson Distinguished Volunteer Award for service to the university. Smith's unwavering dedication to undergraduate education and the financial status of the university has left a marked legacy, one that would be taken in new directions when President Rawlins took the reins in mid-2000.

RESEARCH NOTES

To learn more about the Samuel H. Smith presidency a first stop is the Manuscripts, Archives, and Special Collections (MASC) division of the WSU Libraries located in the Terrell Library on the WSU Pullman campus. MASC contains many boxes of materials from the presidency including speeches given, letters received, events hosted, and goals expressed through 1991. Additionally, MASC contains information on the General Education Curriculum reforms and the activities of the President's Commission on the Status of Women. Almost all the photographs used in this chapter can be found in unprocessed Sam Smith collections or the WSU News collection covering his presidency.

To get an understanding of the student experience at WSU, there are no better sources than issues of the student newspaper the *Daily Evergreen*. These are online and free to access through MASC's digital collections. Additionally, newspaper articles from the *New York Times* and elsewhere helped place the events unfolding at WSU into a larger picture of the era. Some secondary sources, including the wonderful website HistoryLink, devoted to Washington state history, helped provide some context and detail about Smith's presidency.

President Smith graciously allowed two important interviews—one in 2005 with Tim Marsh and one in 2018 with myself. The transcript of the Tim Marsh interview can be found among the oral history documents within the University Archives held at MASC. My interview with Sam Smith is in my possession and is available upon request.

V. Lane Rawlins

2000–2007

BY BUDDY LEVY

WHEN V. LANE RAWLINS ARRIVED IN PULLMAN IN June of 2000 to serve as Washington State University's ninth president, it was a homecoming. Over the previous fourteen years Pullman had grown. There were many new buildings on campus, and the student body population was considerably larger. But he certainly knew the lay of the land, the feel of the campus and the town. As he entered his new office, he had the unique distinction of being the first—and to this day, only—WSU president to have previously been a member of the university's faculty. He also carried with him extensive administrative experience. He had exemplary credentials at the university level, having been a department chair, a vice provost, a vice chancellor, and, most recently, a university president.

Prior to an academic career that spanned five decades, young Lane Rawlins was, in his own words, "raised as an Idaho farm boy should be. On a potato farm." He was born November 30, 1937 in Rexburg, Idaho, to parents Narvel Rawlins and Jennie Brown Rawlins, and brought up in the Mormon faith. Rawlins's parents owned one hundred acres of irrigated land along the South Fork of the Snake River, and their fortunes, according to Rawlins, "depended on weather and the price of potatoes."

It was as simple as that. All of his ancestors were Mormon pioneers who settled in various regions in the West—mostly in southeastern Idaho, in the Teton Basin.

His parents instilled in him a sense of duty, discipline, service, and hard work—both physical and intellectual. Self-described as "hyperactive, and in trouble—not serious trouble, just trouble," Rawlins credits his father's reasonable approach to discipline, his willingness to work things out verbally, in helping him grow. "He wasn't a hard disciplinarian—he used language and reason." Lane's mother Jennie Brown Rawlins read poetry and stories to him, and she was always writing. She was a farm wife and a mother, but she defined herself as a writer. She wrote about a half dozen books, including her first, *High Button Shoes*, published in 1962. (The Jennie Brown Rawlins Scholarship, a $2,000 award given annually through WSU's Department of English, is awarded in her name to the best undergraduate writing in two genres.)

Lane Rawlins first enrolled as a freshman at Ricks College in the fall of 1955 but left shortly to work. He enrolled at Idaho State University in January 1957 and attended until January of 1958. That spring, he embarked on a two-year Mormon mission in Australia, including a year in Tasmania, that would have a profound impact on him. In a number of ways, the experience Down Under played a major role in shaping the leader he was to become.

Rawlins enjoyed his interaction with other missionaries, becoming part of a fairly extensive Mormon community. What inspired him most was teaching religion classes to youngsters in grades 1–8. He discovered that he loved teaching, and especially to youth. He was good at it. People responded to him, and it gave him a sense of pride to hold students' attention and to share knowledge with them.

The two years away affected him intellectually as well as spiritually. While it was a very busy time, there was also ample opportunity for self-reflection. He became more thoughtful and contemplative, posing a lot of questions, and deeply considering his relationship to deity. But much of the time was about preparing, about serving people. It was about reading and conversing and teaching.

Rawlins and wife Mary Jo in a formal portrait, 2003.
WSU News Subject Files, ua333b80f37_cd7077. WSU MASC.

He returned a changed man, more resolute and focused. "When I came home I was very serious. Both because of my time on the mission, but also because I had dated this lovely girl before I went to Australia. And while it wouldn't be accurate to say she just waited for me, she was still there when I got back, and we decided to get married." Things moved fast from there. He transferred to BYU, and he and his wife Mary Jo had two children by the time he graduated in 1963 with a bachelor's degree in economics.

At BYU, Rawlins was fortunate to meet and be mentored by Professor Richard "Dick" Wirthlin, who had received a PhD in economics from Berkeley in 1964 and became the chair of the BYU Department of Economics that year. Wirthlin was known as a brilliant educator who cared deeply about students. He would go on to be appointed campaign director of strategy and planning for the 1980 and 1984 Reagan presidential campaigns. A brilliant and pioneering pollster, he was Reagan's political advisor and confidante, having breakfast with the president nearly every morning. While Rawlins was an undergraduate at BYU, Wirthlin, who clearly saw potential in the young man, approached him and suggested he attend graduate school.

"At the time, I barely knew what graduate school was," said Rawlins.

He would know very soon. He applied to a number of America's finest graduate schools, and was accepted at Harvard, the University of Chicago, the University of Washington, and the University of California, Berkeley. Harvard was prohibitively expensive; Chicago intrigued him, but he had two small children and did not fancy dragging them there to live in a city of that size. He very nearly chose UW—they offered him a great financial package and promised a job for his wife Mary Jo. It was enticing, and he had verbally committed when the economics department at Berkeley called and offered him a fellowship that had opened up. So, he took the fellowship in 1963 and moved to California. (Incidentally, the same year, his predecessor as president of WSU, Samuel Smith, was just finishing his doctorate in plant sciences at the same institution—Smith was Rawlins's predecessor at UC Berkeley, too).

Rawlins wasn't certain how prepared he would be for graduate school. Professor Wirthlin had encouraged him, so that helped, but Rawlins remembered clearly the day he sat down in his first economic theory class. "I introduced myself to the guy on my left, and he had just graduated from Harvard. And I talked to the guy on my right, who had just graduated from Yale. I had a moment where I thought, 'What the hell am I doing here?'" Rawlins joked. "But I'd been taught, 'Everybody puts their pants on one leg at a time.'"

It turned out he was just as prepared as the students from the Ivy League schools, maybe even more so. Rawlins flourished at Berkeley. He found the atmosphere challenging, stimulating, and exciting. He put his nose to the grindstone and did his work. So much was going on socially in the country at the time—race relations, issues of free speech, Vietnam. Kennedy had recently been assassinated. In March of 1965 the first American combat troops landed at China Beach north of Da Nang.

Berkeley students were particularly active. Rawlins remembers reading the famous *Berkeley Barb*, the underground newspaper launched in 1965 by Max Scherr to serve as a leftist voice and their "civil rights, anti-war, and countercultural movements."

During his formative time at Berkeley, Rawlins got to know the fiery and magnetic speaker Mario Savio, an advocate and key member of the Berkeley Free Speech Movement and the leader of Students for a Democratic Society. Rawlins recalled listening to the charismatic figure whose wild, curly hair seemed to stand on end, electrified, when he spoke. Savio remains an icon of that early period in American counterculture. The last year Rawlins was at Berkeley, 1968, was politically volatile. The campus was tear-gassed once. "When Martin Luther King was assassinated, I went out there in the square. And we all sat out, probably 10,000 of us sat there for an hour, in total silence."

With his coursework completed and holding the status of All But Dissertation (ABD), Rawlins applied for jobs, and with his Berkeley credential he got a lot of offers. He wanted to locate somewhere in the Northwest, and took a job offer at Washington State University in 1968 as an assistant professor of economics. He received his PhD from Berkeley in 1969. He and Mary Jo had wanted to be in relatively close proximity to southeastern Idaho where both their parents lived. Pullman suited him well, and in various capacities he would spend the next eighteen years on the Palouse, long before he ever became the university's ninth president.

AS A PROFESSOR, RAWLINS THRIVED. HE TOOK HIS preparation seriously, spending hours on lesson plans and course organization. Initially he found the teaching aspect was difficult, probably because he cared so much. "I was one of those guys who would be pacing back and forth in my office for a half an hour before every class, all keyed up." He wanted to get it right.

Such preparation and dedication paid off. Students gravitated toward his classes. One student named David Knowles says that his life was altered—in ways that would not be fully realized until much later—by his first encounter with Rawlins. "I took his labor economics class in 1968; he was fresh from Berkeley, I was a senior. One class from him and I was hooked—even though I was a political science major. I was enthralled by him. He was persistent, polite, and a skilled presenter of theory. His classroom environment spawned learning. He taught back-handedly. With questions he asked us, with short stories he presented, his classes became pockets of information that attached themselves, surreptitiously, to our minds." Inspired by Rawlins, Knowles went on to earn a PhD in economics from WSU, writing his dissertation under him.

While teaching (and later, while in administration), Rawlins also published prolifically, placing articles widely in major journals such as the *Journal of Human Resources*, *The Monthly Labor Review*, and *The American Economic Review*. He co-authored books, including *Public Service Employment 1976–80* with Robert F. Cook and Charles Adams (W. E. Upjohn, 1986), and *Public Service Employment: A Field Evaluation* with Richard P. Nathan and Robert F. Cook (The Brookings Institution, 1981).

One thing that set Rawlins apart from his peers, especially as a junior professor, was his gregariousness and fearlessness. "Fortunately, I wasn't born with the fear gene." He got to know both Wallis Beasley—who worked at WSU for 33 years, serving as professor, department chair, and interim president—and Glenn Terrell, who was president when Rawlins arrived. "Probably only four or five percent of the young faculty would have that opportunity," Rawlins noted. Rawlins headed up a couple of search committees for Beasley. And the upstart Rawlins was something of a gadfly. Asked how an untenured faculty member got on a first-name basis with one of the higher administrators and the president of the university, Rawlins replied, "Mostly it was because I was such a pain. I wanted to know the budget—they wouldn't release the budget. I got after them. We started organizing, not really a union, but a group that paid dues to hire lobbyists to help lobby for the faculty."

Rawlins worked hard, teaching undergraduate and eventually graduate courses in the economics department. His research, particularly about the effects of job training programs for youth, brought him connections to Washington, DC. With the assistance of inspired and able graduate students, he wrote grants and garnered funds for their research, and got involved as a research associate for the Brookings Institution from 1976 to 1979.

He served as chair of the economics department from 1977 to 1981. During his last year, Washington State University hired Albert C. "Al" Yates as executive vice president and provost, a move Rawlins thought brilliant. Yates worked for WSU for nine years. Rawlins said Yates "was probably more responsible for the progress of the university at that time than anybody else." The university was operating within a tight budget, and under Yates, Rawlins learned much about making tough choices: eliminating unproductive faculty, downsizing programs and departments. Of the provost, Rawlins remarked, "Yates was the smartest man and administrator I ever worked for, absolutely. He was also extremely demanding."

From 1982 to 1986, Rawlins served as vice provost and at the end of that period, he took a job as vice chancellor of the University of Alabama System, a position he held for five years. Part of his decision to go to the south was a desire to get involved in civil rights, the seed of which had been planted during his time at Berkeley. He would remain in the south for the next 15 years.

As vice chancellor he oversaw the entire University of Alabama System, including the campuses in Huntsville, Birmingham, and Tuscaloosa. He liked Alabama and got very involved in the church. "During that time, we started bringing African-Americans into the Mormon church, which was encouraging. We ran into some resistance some places, but overall that was an important time for me."

As vice chancellor in Alabama, Rawlins studied presidents of multiple universities. He paid close attention, observing how they worked. That five years was ample training, so that when in 1991 he was offered the job as president of the University of Memphis, he believed he was ready. And he was. He piloted Memphis for nine years. Mary Jo loved it in Memphis; they had great friends and were involved in the community. Rawlins believed he'd stay there until he retired.

Fortunately for Washington State University, that did not happen. With President Samuel Smith was set to retire after the academic year in 2000, WSU needed to search for a new president. The search committee called Lane Rawlins and asked him if he'd consider being a candidate. He told them no. Then they asked him if he'd at least be willing to come and consult with them about what they needed in a candidate—after all, Rawlins had already been a professor, a department chair, and vice provost at WSU. Rawlins agreed to that, but once he got to WSU for meetings, he realized they had considered him a candidate all along. They offered him the job. His mother and sister had both moved to the state of Washington by then, and it felt like the right move to make—he hadn't been living near his family since 1986, and it would be good to come back to the West. It would be good to come home.

AFTER OFFICIALLY TAKING THE POSITION ON JUNE 8, 2000, Rawlins rolled up his sleeves and got to work. There was much to do. On arriving, he was somewhat shocked to learn that the image of WSU remained that of a "party school." He instituted external research statewide and follow-up focus groups aimed directly at prospective students and parents. Broad perceptions of the university remained negative and included references to riots, underperforming students, and allusions to lack of safety. Changing the public reputation of the university was one of the biggest challenges he faced in the early years of his presidency, a problem complicated by the fact that the university was at the time under-enrolled, which had precipitated accepting students whose academic achievement was not as high as Rawlins wanted to see.

To deal with these challenges, Rawlins made a number of strong initial moves that illustrated his unique leadership style as delegator. At the University of Memphis, he'd tried to run everything all by himself,

Retiring President Sam
Smith greets Lane Rawlins
in February 2000.
*WSU News Subject Files,
ua333b80f37. WSU MASC.*

but he learned that the boss/worker environment is less effective than a
team environment. It takes more work, it takes more meetings, but in the
end, Rawlins found that delegation is much more effective: empowering
small teams to go out and get work done energizes them and achieves
results. Give them direction but trust their innovativeness and creativity.

Rawlins employed an unconventional technique to inspire the teams
he created. He had a poster of a meerkat family on the wall in his office.
Meerkats are weasel-like animals, part of the mongoose family, known
for living in tight-knit units and working collaboratively. The poster
depicted a group of them, all standing on their two hind feet, looking
in the same direction, eyes wide open, alert. In meetings, Rawlins would
talk about how meerkats depend on each other, how it takes an entire
community to make things happen, and how each meerkat had a specific
role but they all relied on one another. He used the meerkat metaphor
often, and it had a positive impact on his employees.

To embody the meerkat model, Rawlins appointed faculty and staff
to a series of nine "design teams" whose task was to set major goals

Rawlins at Bryan Tower, June 2000. *Historic WSU Photographs Collection, pc004b36. WSU MASC.*

and objectives for the next 5–10 years as part of an overall strategic plan that would address myriad areas of perceived need, including the undergraduate experience, athletics, the role of branch campuses, and diversity, both among the student body and the faculty. The design teams were comprehensive and ambitious. Comprised of 8–10 members each, they would meet and report progress regularly. One of Rawlins's great leadership attributes was his ability to listen to what the teams reported to him, and act accordingly. An initial skeptic of this long-term strategic planning was provost Dr. Ron Hopkins. Rawlins says that one of his best days on the job was some years later when Hopkins conceded that his approach seemed to be working. The four strategic goals of the design teams were clear: 1: Offer the best undergraduate experience in a research university; 2: Nurture a world-class environment for research, scholarship, graduate education, the arts, and engagement; 3: Create an environment of trust and respect in all we do; 4: Develop a culture of shared commitment to quality in all of our activities.

Rawlins believed that one of the most important aspects of a university is its reputation. He wanted to change the image of WSU and to attract more highly qualified students and enhance the undergraduate student education, including building and sustaining a more diverse student body as well as a more diverse faculty. Rawlins also wanted to raise the academic standards of WSU. On more than one occasion, when he asked a particular student why they decided to come to WSU, they told him it was because they couldn't get into some other school, like UW, Evergreen, or Western. He did not want to hear that *ever* again.

So, he tasked an identity design team to work on it. The internal team hired a consulting PR firm to help with the rebranding. They put the famous Cougar head, designed in 1936 by then WSU student Randall Johnson, back on merchandise, pins, literature, catalogues, pamphlets, letterhead—anything and everything related to WSU. They had design meetings about the colors, too. In one meeting, they showed Rawlins the colors—a new and more vibrant crimson and gray, on a white background. He told them he didn't much care for them. The identity design team responded by saying, "That's good, because we're not really trying to recruit too many 65-year-old guys!" Rawlins just laughed and let them do their work. That fall, on November 17, 2000, WSU unveiled its new graphic identity at a Board of Regents meeting held in Spokane. The identity design team was also responsible for coming up with the motto "World Class, Face to Face," which underscored WSU's reputation as one of the nation's leading public research institutions.

The PR firm pushed hard to try to eliminate the nickname "Wazzu," which had gained widespread use. Rawlins agreed that the term was inappropriate and unhelpful. But the expression was too deeply ingrained to eradicate, no matter how hard they tried. There were pockets of resistance everywhere. Rawlins wasn't overly fixated on it; he just didn't think it helped the university's image. At one commencement, after graduating, the student body president handed President Rawlins a T-shirt that had "Wazzu" emblazoned across the front, and he had to laugh. It was all in good fun, and there were bigger battles to fight.

THE REGENTS SCHOLARS PROGRAM, CONCEIVED OF IN 2000 and which continues today, was a huge step in recruiting and retaining the highest quality students from across the state of Washington. The idea was to offer significant scholarships to outstanding students whose cumulative GPAs and SAT or ACT scores met certain stringent requirements. To qualify, graduating seniors would need a minimum GPA of 3.5 and an SAT score of 1200 or ACT score of 25. The eligibility had a sliding scale—the higher the GPA of the applicant, there was a slight lowering for their required standardized test scores. Rawlins's hope was to send a strong message that the best students from high schools all across the state of Washington should choose WSU over all of their options. To promote the new program, Rawlins himself, as well as recruiters, went to communities all around Washington, visiting schools, hosting distinguished alumni and donors, and working to spread the word about this excellent opportunity. They also raised money to pay for the scholarships.

The program was, and continues to be, highly successful. In December of 2001 the university announced its first class of 25 recipients, whose group average GPA was 3.97 and SAT average was 1300. They were a diverse group of achievers that included musicians, varsity athletes, National Honor Society members, student body presidents, and National Merit Finalists. They received scholarships of $14,000 per year, and the prestigious awards were renewable for four years (provided the student maintained a 3.0 GPA at the Pullman campus, taking at least 24 credits per year), making the total package worth $56,000 per student at that time.

One of the first recipients, Steffany McGowan Kraft, has said that without question, receiving the Regents Scholarship set her life on its course. She had been mostly interested in California schools, but when she learned about this fantastic scholarship opportunity, it swayed her. The Regents Scholarship molded her into "an educated, critical-thinking, engaged citizen." The Regents Scholars Program worked exceptionally well from its inception. By fall 2003, the university enrolled its most pre-pared freshman class in history, with 15 National Merit Scholar Finalists and 25 Distinguished Regents Scholars. This helped set the tone that WSU would be an excellent first choice for high achieving students.

WHEN RAWLINS TOOK THE REINS OF THE PRESIDENCY in 2000, he inherited an athletics program in some disarray. Men's football and basketball, the two largest revenue generators as well as big recruiting draws, were floundering. There were rumors that WSU might be disinvited from the conference under the forthcoming PAC 10 realignment. The football team, in the two previous years under Mike Price, had gone 3–8 and 3–9 (though Price had taken the Cougars to the 1997 Rose Bowl), and the basketball team had gone 10–19 and 10–19 under Kevin Eastman, finishing last in the PAC 10 both seasons. Rawlins, a lifelong sports fan, wanted change. Though he had long had doubts about "the massive athletic enterprises attached to institutions of higher learning," he accepted early on that he was not going to change that, so he decided the best he could do was keep sports fair, positive, and focused on the experience of the student athlete. To do so, he got involved. He got to know every coach who ever served under him and told them bluntly that if they abused their athletes in any way, or if they deliberately broke the rules, they were gone. Rawlins also sat on the bench or stood on the sidelines during games and got to know many of the athletes. He told his coaches it was important that the kids knew the university cared about them and their experience as student athletes.

While in the south, Rawlins had been chair of the Great Mid-West Conference (1994–95), chair of Conference USA (1995–96), and he would eventually chair the PAC-10 Conference in his final year at WSU (2006–2007). He served on the NCAA Board of Directors for five years (1996–2000, 2006–2007), so his involvement with college athletics was considerable. At WSU, the first major move Rawlins made was to hire Jim Sterk as athletic director in 2000, snagging him from his position at Portland State. Sterk's background in athletic administration and his familiarity with the northwest made him an ideal hire. Sterk would remain at WSU until 2010, bolstering many of the school's programs, the so-called "non-revenue sports" as well as revenue sports, and gaining national notoriety. The Cougar football team made the Rose Bowl in the 2002 season (losing to Oklahoma 34–14) and won the Holiday Bowl in 2003, beating Texas 28–20.

Sterk will never forget one of the first meetings he had with Rawlins. Rawlins is a large presence, physically and in bearing; he is tall and can seem rather imposing, despite his kindly nature. Sterk was in his office and they were discussing the athletics budget, which as an economist, Rawlins managed and oversaw. Sterk recalled Rawlins saying, "Jim, here's the budget and here's how it works: you need to stay within your budget. If you go over, we can work on it and figure it out. But if you go over twice, you're fired." Sterk wasn't sure whether his president was joking or not, but it set the tone, and they had a terrific working relationship.

Under Rawlins's watchful eye, Sterk pushed WSU athletics in new directions. The WSU Football team enjoyed three 10-win seasons from 2001 to 2003 (two under Coach Mike Price and one under Coach Bill Doba). But it was Sterk's ingenious basketball hiring of the Bennetts—father Dick in 2003 and son Tony in 2006—for which Sterk will be most remembered. In March of 2003, Sterk announced that he'd enticed coaching legend Dick Bennett out of retirement to come to WSU, with the understanding that his son Tony Bennett would succeed him as head coach when Dick retired. In a story that has become Cougar lore, Sterk knew that Dick Bennett loved golf, so he drove the Bennetts to Coeur

Rawlins at the All-Campus Picnic in 2000.
Historic WSU Photographs Collection, pc004b36. WSU MASC.

d'Alene to show them the course and the resort. The next day, he drove them down through Idaho all the way to Lewiston, showing them the UI course and the courses in Lewiston/Clarkston to convince them—but primarily Dick—that there were excellent golf courses nearby, and that he could play year-round. That sealed the deal. Dick Bennett helped shore up and rebuild during his three-year stint, but Tony Bennett took the Cougar basketball program to new heights: two consecutive 26-win seasons (2006–2007 and 2007–2008) which were both school records, and two consecutive trips to the NCAA tournament. In his second year at WSU, Tony Bennett won the prestigious Henry Iba Award, recognizing the college basketball coach of the year.

Rawlins was instrumental in spearheading significant improvements on the facilities side of athletics, too. He and Sterk agreed that Martin Stadium was not up to PAC-10 standards. There were sections of the stadium lined by ugly chain link fence, and you could see porta-potties through the mesh. Martin Stadium had not undergone a major renovation since 1979 (though it was re-turfed for $288,000 in 2006). In 2007 Martin Stadium's seating capacity was the lowest in the PAC-10 at 35,117.

Rawlins supported a four-phase $55 million renovation plan. Phase one included the beautification of the stadium's east and south ends, with new restroom facilities, larger walkways, and updated concession stands. Phase two would expand the northern concourse area and phases three and four would add premium seating and an additional 2,200 seats. The project continued on and would ultimately be fully realized during the presidency of Elson Floyd.

Another indelible mark left by President Rawlins was the Palouse Ridge Golf Club. The original golf course was built in the 1930s and renovated in the 1970s. For over two decades, there had been ongoing discussions between various factions in WSU administration, the Board of Regents, and the community about the potential benefits of having a championship-level golf course connected to the WSU campus. Part of the impetus was that the existing course was not up to PAC-10 standards, so both the men's and women's golf teams often practiced in Clarkston/Lewiston. Also, WSU could not host home tournaments on the nine-hole campus course as it was too short.

The proposed expansion was controversial from the start. Environmental groups like the Center for Environmental Law & Policy opposed the idea because the Grande Ronde Aquifer—the primary source of water for the cities of Pullman, Washington, and Moscow, Idaho (and for both university campuses)—had experienced declining levels at a rate of about two feet per year for several decades. This group and concerned community members argued that adding nine more holes to the existing course would increase water usage from roughly 15 million gallons per year to irrigate 35 acres to a potential 125 million gallons per year to irrigate the expanded course on the proposed 315-acre site. WSU's Capital Planning Department projected a much smaller number, estimating use of 30–55 million gallons per year. (The 2015 Water System Plan Update

for WSU cited an average of 45 million gallons.) Rawlins and the Board
of Regents were convinced that a new irrigation system could minimize
the water consumption to an acceptable number.

There were other considerations. An upgraded course would increase
alumni, visitor, and conference participation. A championship-level course
would allow WSU to host PAC-10 tournaments (and potentially even
NCAA tournaments) and be an excellent tool for recruiting and retention. Rawlins, himself a golfer, argued that if they were going to pursue
the project, it would be important to build a course that complemented
the terrain, used native grasses, and reduced the overall environmental
footprint, protecting open spaces like Round Top Park, a small campus
park. If designed right, the course could also include outdoor academic
instructional areas for environmental sciences and turf sciences. The plan
was to pay for the course—an estimated $8.5 million—using private funds.

On October 22, 2004, the Board of Regents approved a plan to
construct the new 18-hole championship course and practice facility on
the Pullman campus. Less than four years later, on August 29, 2008, on
a calm day under clear skies, Palouse Ridge Golf Club officially opened.
The course was designed by John Harbottle III, known for producing
rolling links layouts that blended seamlessly into their natural environment, preserving the natural resources, wildlife habitat, and scenic beauty
of the given landscape. Harbottle took advantage of the Palouse hills,
whose rolling, dune-like undulations are a legacy of the last ice age and
the cumulative effect of tens of thousands of years of wind-blown dust
and silt, known as "loess," from the dry regions of the channeled scab-
lands to the southwest.

The 7,308-yard layout, patterned after many of the classic links-style
courses in Scotland, offered expansive views and tremendous challenge
for golfers. Amenities now include a 20-acre practice facility, an off-season
indoor practice facility, a 5,000 square foot event pavilion, a fully stocked
golf shop, and Banyans on the Ridge—a full-service, gourmet restaurant
open seven days a week. The course was voted the #2 Best College Campus Course in 2014 by *Golf Links Magazine*, and "Best Course You Can

Rawlins and students chat on the grass above the Terrell Library. *Historic WSU Photographs Collection, pc004b36. WSU MASC.*

Play" 2009–2015 by *Golfweek Magazine*. The award-winning golf course has hosted numerous marquee events, including the Pac-12 Women's Championships in 2012, the NCAA Men's Division I Regional in 2013, and the Pac-12 Men's Championships in 2015. Palouse Ridge Golf Club has become a defining element of WSU, and a beautiful lasting testament to Rawlins, who had the audacity to champion it.

RAWLINS HAS HAD A LIFETIME INTEREST IN DIVERSITY and equality issues. Certainly this awareness was expanded in the volatile time when he was a PhD student at Berkeley, and equal rights

issues were the reason he wanted to move to the south, where he hoped
to make some difference. At WSU, Rawlins set up focus groups and
listened to the concerns of his design teams, students, and faculty. He
determined that the university needed to do a much better job in areas
of diversity. The Diversity Education Initiative, begun in 2002, instituted
guest lectures in classrooms, short courses, study circles, and training
focused on intercultural communication skills, conflict management,
and multicultural competence. In 2003–2004, Rawlins noticed that
women represented about 44 percent of assistant professors at WSU,
35 percent of associate professors, and 13 percent of full professors. Again,
he thought the university needed to do better. He created a Council
for the Advancement of Women, aimed at improving opportunities for
women in senior faculty positions, particularly in engineering, math, and
science. By 2008, the year following Rawlins's tenure at WSU, women
represented 19% of full and Regents Professors and 40% of associate
professors, so his programs definitely had an impact.

Rawlins was just getting started. In 2004 Rawlins created the Commission on Race and Ethnicity, and in June of that year hired Michael J.
Tate to serve as the university's interim vice president for equity and
diversity. The goal was clear: to increase diversity on the WSU campuses,
especially among faculty and staff. By national standards, Rawlins was
an early adopter of diversity concerns. A 2006 article in the *Chronicle of
Higher Education* called "The Rise of the Chief Diversity Officer," noted
President Lane Rawlins's foresight and sensitivity to diversity issues.
By 2006 Tate had an annual budget of $3 million and a full-time staff
of 55 and was offering diversity training to more than 1,000 people at
WSU. Under Tate, the Office of Equity and Diversity also began reno-
vating existing historic university houses to convert into cultural centers
for Hispanic and African American students. As of 2018, there existed
four such houses: Asian Pacific American Cultural House, Casa Latina,
Native American Cultural House, and Talmadge Anderson Heritage
House. The diversity and equity initiatives and programs created under
Rawlins continued after his term. By fall of 2017, 33.3 percent of the

freshman class came from ethnically diverse/minority backgrounds, up from just 12 percent in 2008.

ONE OF THE THINGS RAWLINS IS PROUDEST OF IS THAT he came to be known as "The Faculty's President." This title was well earned through his interactions with faculty and also in his creation of events and awards that honored and recognized faculty. When he arrived, he decided to institute an event of celebration, one he'd conceived at the University of Memphis that had worked well. It was a way of acknowledging the merits and achievements of faculty (and later, of undergraduates and graduate/professional students) in a public setting. At WSU, Showcase began in 2003 as a one or two day event highlighting faculty achievement and included a luncheon featuring a distinguished speaker. It culminated in an evening faculty awards banquet. This event has grown into the week-long Showcase forum for sharing research, scholarship, and creative work with the WSU community.

Now held each year in the Compton Union Building, Showcase attracts faculty, staff, and graduate/professional students from all campuses, disciplines, and Extension offices statewide to the Pullman campus. There is a poster session where scholars' work is on display, a Distinguished Faculty Address honoring a faculty member whose work represents the highest levels in their discipline, and a culminating "Celebrating Excellence Banquet," a dinner honoring the outstanding achievements of WSU faculty and staff. Numerous honors are presented during the evening, including the V. Lane Rawlins Lifetime Service Award, the President's Distinguished Teaching Award for Non–Tenure Track Faculty, the Sahlin Faculty Excellence Awards, and the Faculty Diversity Award, among others. At the event, newly tenured and/or promoted faculty are also recognized. The week-long festivity has grown to include Crimson Reads: A Celebration of WSU Authors, and the president's State of the University address, which is held in Bryan

Auditorium. The Showcase remains a major annual event, growing bigger, more dynamic, and better attended every year.

The three additional WSU "branch campuses" initiated under President Samuel Smith were strengthened and further developed under President Rawlins. The campuses in Spokane, the Tri-Cities, and Vancouver had been formalized through legislative process in 1989 and shored up under President Samuel Smith, but there remained work to be done. Rawlins believed that each institution should have its own identity and reflect particular strengths and attributes of its location. But it would take long-term strategic planning, which ended up being a defining element of Rawlins's leadership style. Buttressing the branch campuses would require listening to the communities where the campuses resided and gaining a more direct access to the highest levels of administration at these campuses. Rawlins, with deep hands-on support from the Board of Regents, became actively involved in framing the direction of the branch campuses. In 2003, the WSU regents gave the deans of the urban campuses in Spokane, Tri-Cities, and Vancouver the title of "chancellor" and expanded their responsibilities. One of these responsibilities was reporting directly to President Rawlins, which was very important to him.

The Vancouver campus was quite established and growing well, and Rawlins determined that the branch could offer a complete array of programs, including bachelor's degrees, graduate degrees, minors, and certificates. Tri-Cities, with a smaller population base, presented enrollment challenges. Rawlins went to the Tri-Cities, held a community-wide forum on the Richland campus in November 2004, and, along with Tri-Cities Chancellor Larry James, discussed the future of WSU Tri-Cities and listened to the needs of the community. The planned direction would focus on the prominent industries in the area: the winery and viticulture industries, and the region's long-established connection to Hanford and the Pacific Northwest National Laboratory. The close ties and associations also provided tremendous research and internship access to students. As such, two of the most rigorous and effective programs at

WSU Tri-Cities today are Viticulture & Enology (Wine Science) and Engineering/Applied Science.

At WSU Spokane, the focus would be on the health sciences, which made sense given Spokane's position as an established, vital medical hub in the Inland Northwest. Rawlins and the Board of Regents made the decision to move the pharmacy school there, and in February 2002 the Health Sciences Building opened. The 145,000-square-foot building was state-of-the-art, comprising clinical spaces, offices, classrooms, and wet and dry labs. One of Rawlins's grand ideas was to form a joint medical school with the University of Washington, in which the programs would be UW's, but the faculty would primarily be from WSU. The concept did not work out, but the commitment to a health science presence in Spokane was firmly rooted, and that focus developed even further under Rawlins's successor Elson S. Floyd, for whom the college of medicine is now named.

WHEN RAWLINS "RETIRED" IN 2007, HE HANDED THE leadership over to the more than able Floyd. But Rawlins didn't actually retire. He returned to the WSU faculty in the WSU School of Economics, and shortly afterwards, became interim director of the William D. Ruckelshaus Center for Conflict Resolution, in which role he served from 2007 to 2009. The center is a joint venture between Washington State University (hosted and administered by the WSU Extension) and the University of Washington (hosted through the Daniel J. Evans School of Public Policy and Governance), a collaboration seeking shared solutions to complex public policy issues in the state of Washington and the Pacific Northwest.

In 2010 the indefatigable Rawlins accepted an interim position as president of the University of North Texas. Within a year, at the request of the chancellor and regents of UNT, he extended his contract and served until his last retirement in 2014, as president emeritus. It was his

Rawlins and students on campus.
Historic WSU Photographs Collection, pc004b36. WSU MASC.

third university presidency, and by that time he was 77. Rawlins settled in Lewiston, Idaho, with his wife Mary Jo, and they continued to be vital regional community members. As of 2018, President Rawlins still kept a small office in Hulbert Hall that he occasionally used when on campus.

The legacy of President V. Lane Rawlins is felt throughout the campuses today. People who worked with him described the experience as "energizing and inspiring," citing his steadfast devotion to the students and the university above all else. When making tough decisions, he was known to ask this simple question: "Is it good for the students?" If the answer was "no," then he believed WSU should not do it. He was guided by two central elements: research and undergraduate education. "That's what the university is supposed to be about," believed Rawlins. "That's what E. A. Bryan conceived it to be. He was our father, and I have no quarrel with his vision."

Cosmetic enhancements took place under Rawlins's tenure, like landscaping along Stadium Way, new signage for campus buildings, the evolution of Library Road into a pedestrian-friendly plaza, and even sometimes-controversial public art, like Jim Dine's *Technicolor Heart* near the intersection of Stadium Way and Grimes Way. Rawlins's legacy can also be seen in a number of buildings, like the Shock Physics Building and the V. Lane Rawlins Research and Education Complex, several interconnected life science research buildings (Vogel Plant Sciences, Biotechnology and Life Sciences, and Veterinary and Biomedical Research). This complex is a fitting tribute to a man who devoted five decades to academics and higher education and who, in his final State of the University address—given September 27, 2006—said "For us the destination is becoming increasingly clear. We want to be and can be one of the elite institutions in the world in both education and research." That was what he called his North Star, and his vision remained fixed on it throughout his presidency.

RESEARCH NOTES

The central sources for this chapter on V. Lane Rawlins were personal interviews conducted between December 2017 and July 2018. Two of the interviews, done at the Rawlins home in December 2017 and via phone in July 2018, will be available as audio recordings and as transcripts at the Manuscripts, Archives, and Special Collections (MASC) division of the WSU Libraries. The author and Lane Rawlins also corresponded frequently through email during the spring and summer of 2018.

The author also conducted email and phone interviews with three key people who worked directly with President Rawlins: Mary Gresch, Jim Sterk, and Warwick Bayly. Mary Gresch, then the director of marketing communications at WSU, provided valuable insight into the design teams Rawlins created and into the working atmosphere fostered by Rawlins. Jim Sterk, athletic director from 2000 to 2010, was interviewed by phone (on May 14, 2018) and by email again in July 2018. Warwick Bayle was interviewed on the WSU Pullman campus on May 14, 2018.

The *Daily Evergreen* was useful for context during Rawlins's tenure. It can be found online through MASC's digital collections. Additionally, newspaper articles from the *Spokesman Review*, the *Seattle Times*, the *Lewiston Morning Tribune*, and the *Moscow-Pullman Daily News* were helpful. *WSU News* and the *WSU Insider* were tremendously useful resources, as was the 2002–2007 Strategic Plan and Progress Reports, available at strategicplan.wsu.edu/archives/2002–2007.

Incidentally, the author has worked at WSU continuously in the Department of English since 1988, so was on campus during Rawlins's entire tenure (as well as all but three years of Sam Smith's, all of Elson Floyd's, and each, so far, of Kirk Schulz's . . .).

Elson S. Floyd
2006–2015

BY PAUL PITRE, AARON NGOZI OFORLEA,
AND BRIAN DIXON

I have learned that success is to be measured
not so much by the position that one has
reached in life as by the obstacles
which he has overcome while
trying to succeed.

BOOKER T. WASHINGTON
UP FROM SLAVERY

ELSON S. FLOYD WAS NAMED WASHINGTON STATE
University's tenth president on December 13, 2006. As president,
he transformed WSU's five campuses by increasing access, affordability,
and quality of education. In the midst of his presidency, he passed away
on June 20, 2015.

On February 29, 1956, Elson Sylvester Floyd was born in the small
racially segregated town of Henderson, North Carolina, less than an
hour's drive from the state capital. For most of his life, he would celebrate his birthday on March 1. As the oldest of four sons, he was raised
by his mother, Dorothy, a third-shift tobacco factory worker and his
father Elson, a brick mason and U.S. Army veteran. Although both

left school to help with their families' finances, his parents embraced a strong work ethic, including waking their sons at 5:30 a.m. to work, run, or swim. In addition, they taught their sons that education makes a difference in one's quality of life. Taking their advice, Floyd studied hard and began reading before kindergarten by borrowing books from the "colored section" of the segregated Dunbar Library. Without the money to afford paper, he practiced mathematics in a sand box near his home. His upbringing and commitment to education transformed him into the first African American president of three universities, a visionary leader, and a skilled statesman.

The Pursuit of Education

Wisdom more than Knowledge;
Service beyond Self;
Honor above Everything.

DARLINGTON SCHOOL MOTTO

After completing elementary school, Floyd received an academic scholarship to attend the Darlington School, a prestigious boarding and college prep school located in Rome, Georgia. As a student, he was confident, competitive, self-determined, and had an immediate impact on his new environment. Bill Smith, Floyd's roommate at Darlington, said "His style and grace were at the forefront of everything he undertook at the Lakeside. Elson made Darlington better simply by his presence." Floyd flourished in leadership at the school, becoming president of the student council, vice president of the Honor Council, a three-sport athlete (track, basketball, football), co-captain of the football team, and voted class favorite by his peers. What the Darlington School meant to Floyd was plain, as was the contribution that he gave to the prestigious boarding school: "Dr. Floyd credited Darlington with changing the trajectory of his life, and it is our honor to memorialize him by dedicating something so significant in his honor," said Head of School Brent Bell at a ceremony

Elson Floyd, at left, at Darlington School.

to memorialize Floyd. Darlington School named a focal point at Silver Lake, on which the school is located, after the late president. For those who knew Elson S. Floyd, the Darlington Motto was what he lived by.

THE COLLEGE YEARS:
UNIVERSITY OF NORTH CAROLINA

As a society, we should not waste
human potential. How can we put
a value on research not done
or teachers who are kept out
of teaching for lack of education?

ELSON S. FLOYD

After graduating from Darlington in 1974, Floyd turned down a football scholarship to accept an academic scholarship in his home state at the University of North Carolina at Chapel Hill (UNC). Before graduating with his bachelor's degree in political science and speech during the spring of 1978, Floyd became one of the founding members of the Alpha Phi Alpha Fraternity at UNC. Floyd earned a master's degree (1982), and a doctorate in adult education (1984). In 1978 Floyd began a career in higher education at his alma mater. After holding several executive leadership positions at UNC, Floyd joined the faculty at Eastern Washington University (EWU). Following promotion to executive vice president at EWU, Floyd left to become the executive director of the Higher Education Coordinating Board (HECB) in Olympia, Washington, the state agency that is responsible for coordinating statewide higher education planning, policy analysis, and student financial aid programs for the Washington state post-secondary education system. He served as executive director of the HECB for two years before returning to UNC to serve as chief administrative and operations officer and the senior official responsible for business and finance, human resources, auxiliary enterprises, student affairs, information technology, university advancement and development, and enrollment management.

In 1998 Floyd was appointed to his first presidency at Western Michigan University (WMU), serving until 2003. There, his legacy includes purchasing the land for and developing the WMU Oakland Drive campus and developing the Parkview campus, which is the home of the Engineering Complex, Business Technology, and Research Park. He gained the support of the Carnegie Foundation to move WMU into the category of Doctoral/Research–Extensive. He also held a tenured faculty position in the Department of Counselor Education and Counseling Psychology and the Department of Teaching, Learning and Leadership.

From fall 2003 until the spring of 2007, Floyd served as the first African American president for the University of Missouri system. Again, his leadership was a primary feature as he steered the university through a financial crisis that included budget cuts and a $400 million lawsuit. His presence was immediately felt throughout Missouri. Former Chief of Staff David R. Russell stated that Floyd brought a special energy: "We came away with a better appreciation for the powerful traits that had endeared Elson to Michigan and would later secure his place in Missouri, and places like Washington state and our nation's capital, as one of the nation's foremost advocates for education and opportunity for all."

Along with a history of success in higher education, Floyd maintained an active family life with his wife Carmento, daughter Jessica, and son Kenny. He and Carmento made a powerful team as they guided the growth and development of three major universities. Furthermore, they contributed their knowledge to many boards and organizations, such as the American Council on Education's Commission on Leadership and Institutional Effectiveness, President George W. Bush's advisory board for the White House Initiative on Historically Black Colleges and Universities, and the Association of Public Land-Grant Universities. Floyd also chaired the Pac-12 CEO Group in the 2014–2015 academic year.

A HERO'S RETURN

I flat out have the best job in the country.
There is something special about WSU and
even more special about being a Coug.
It's about family taking care of family.

ELSON S. FLOYD

In Joseph Campbell's documentary, *A Hero's Journey,* the hero must always leave a familiar setting in order to follow a new path that leads to growth and transformation. Then, after reaching new heights of growth and development, the hero returns. This describes the story of Elson S. Floyd and his journey to Washington, away from Washington, and then back again. In an interview, Floyd said serving as WSU President was "a homecoming" as "I'm very familiar with the state of Washington." WSU officials agreed that although Floyd wasn't a native son of Washington, he understood the diverse cultures, the needs of the student body, and the philosophical underpinnings of successful leadership in higher education in Washington state and the nation.

With ringing endorsements from his predecessor Lane Rawlins and leading members of the Faculty Senate, Floyd was appointed president of WSU. President Rawlins announced to a crowd that he and Floyd shared the same vision. Therefore, Rawlins declared, "if you lifted me up . . . lift him up higher." Ken Struckmeyer, former Faculty Senate chair, and Charles Pezeshki, also a former chair of the Faculty Senate and a member of the presidential search committee, declared that Floyd was "the best candidate out of a great field."

Besides committing to increasing WSU's endowment, he also committed to continuing to improve the student experience including recruiting students within and outside Washington and spending time listening to students' concerns. Students were happy with their new president. Many developed special relationships with Floyd and affectionately referred to him as "EFlo," a nickname he acquired during his years in Missouri. Floyd often went out of his way to greet and visit with each student he encountered. He quickly learned many of their names; and always promised to work hard to guarantee that they felt visible, supported, and appreciated at WSU. To Floyd, students were more than demographics on a college campus; they were a part of the family, the WSU family. He created a family dynamic with many small acts of kindness and generosity including increasing the number of available grants and scholarships that could be used to address individual needs that directly impacted educational experiences. Floyd was known to be generous, kind, and student-centered. It was rumored that at one of his former institutions Floyd showed up to work only wearing socks with no shoes. As the story goes, he had given his boots to a student who was having trouble walking on campus in the snow because of improper shoes.

Elson and his wife, Carmento, attended many student-centered activities, including WSU sports events where they were known to cheer from the student section. Thousands of students followed a Twitter account Dr. Floyd started as a way to better connect with them. He gave many students his personal cell phone number and encouraged them to contact him if they needed anything. In addition, Floyd was known to wait at the hospital with ill students until their parents arrived and invited students to the presidential house for home-cooked meals. Floyd once joked that the "president's mansion is government housing that belongs to everyone."

Floyd, center, points to someone he knows in the student section before Washington State's NCAA college basketball game against UCLA on Saturday, March 5, 2011, in Pullman. *Dean Hare / Fr158448 Ap.*

The Floyd Master Plan

Leaders are defined by their legacy,
which is shaped over time from decisions
they must often make . . . At such
critical choice points, great leaders
access the wizard's mastery of the
symbols and the warrior's command of power.

BOLMAN AND DEAL

THE WIZARD AND THE WARRIOR

Floyd articulated a clear goal of increasing the visibility and stature of the university. In his first address to the university community, Floyd said his goal was to create "a global, world-class land-grant institution."

One of his measures of success would be gaining admission to the American Association of Universities (AAU), an organization comprised of sixty-two distinguished research universities across the United States. AAU universities receive the majority of competitively awarded federal funding for academic research and have domestic as well as international research projects. They have some of the most competitive admissions standards for students, healthy endowments, and the most productive research faculty on the planet, but there isn't an application for AAU status and no clear metrics for becoming a member. "It's sort of an elite club," he noted.

Some of the opportunities Floyd charged WSU to pursue were directly from the university's strategic plan, while some were new opportunities that developed along the way, and others were part of the tactical process to gain AAU status.

Some of the strategic partnerships upon which WSU embarked included a focus on bioenergy and sustainability, a collaboration with the Pacific Northwest National Laboratory through WSU Tri-Cities, and serving the vibrant and diverse cultures and communities in Spokane through WSU's medical center partnership with the University of Washington to contribute to groundbreaking research in the health sciences. WSU Pullman continued to strengthen its research agenda in agriculture, and the Paul G. Allen School for Global Animal Health, committed to eradicating zoonotic diseases (diseases transmitted from animals to humans), was founded. WSU Vancouver brought a comprehensive, research focused approach to southwest Washington, as a critical component of the WSU system.

Reflecting on how Floyd moved Washington State University in the direction of AAU status, Mike Worthy, former chair of the WSU Board of Regents, commented that Floyd "convinced us just how great we [could] be." Echoing Worthy, Provost Dan Bernardo said, "his initiative was the realization that WSU is the provider of education and research-based solutions to the grand challenges of this state. He liked to say we were 'Washington state's university.'"

Just as he began pursuing his goal of moving WSU down the path of becoming one of the nation's premiere land-grant universities, President Floyd encountered the worst national economic recession in fifty years. His response to the economic downturn included a dramatic reconceptualization of the WSU system. He resolved not to allow the financial crisis to hinder students from receiving a world-class education. For once the crises ended, Floyd believed that students would need robust educational tools to help them build their lives and careers. Floyd's reconceptualization included highlighting areas of strength, building solid partnerships, and focusing on fundraising, improving technology, and reaching underserved communities.

Despite the financial crises, President Floyd pushed forward with plans for building the reputation and national standing of WSU. His plan for raising the stature of WSU was three-pronged. First, he would build a medical school. Second, he would expand WSU to the west side of the state to broaden its appeal. Finally, he would work to raise one billion dollars to solidify the long-term future of WSU.

In addition to the aforementioned aspirational initiatives, Floyd ushered in a new era for WSU Athletics, and transformed the WSU Pullman into a contemporary, competitively accessorized, tier 1 research university campus. Working on that premise, Floyd sought to move WSU to be more in line with its peer institutions. For example, all of the (then) Pac-10 universities had combined colleges of arts and sciences except for Oregon State University and the University of Arizona. Additionally, 17 of WSU's 22 peer institutions had similarly combined colleges of arts and sciences. Floyd saw the wisdom in that change and instituted it at WSU.

THE BUDGET CRISIS AND PRIORITIZATION

Let me be clear: we must protect our academic priorities;
we must protect our current employees, and we must
never apply budget reductions across the board
for to do so puts us in a circumstance of mediocrity,
and mediocrity is unacceptable.

ELSON S. FLOYD

As Washington and the nation entered an economic tailspin, Washington State University entered an era of cost-cutting and retrenchment. At that moment, the university had been committed to the process of program prioritization to focus attention on growing academic and research programs that had the potential for expanding or gaining national prominence through additional faculty, program development, research funding, and graduate and undergraduate students. This process, named the Academic Affairs Program Prioritization (A2P2) required colleges and units to look closely at programs to determine their scalability and viability. More specifically, programs were asked to do self-evaluations to determine their future trajectory. Each program was then classified in one of three categories: 1. Grow/invest, 2. Sustain, or 3. Downsize/reorganize.

The A2P2 process quickly shifted from a resource allocation process, aimed at increasing WSU's stature and strengthening programs, to a budget-cutting exercise aimed at stopping the bleeding and patching the budget gaps left by decreasing state financial support. The mood at the time of the A2P2 process was one of disbelief—disbelief that the continuous cuts to the university budget by the state had no end in sight. Many doubted the severity of the national budget crisis, and the devastating effect that it was having on the state of Washington and its residents. Continuous budget shortfalls were cascading down upon institutions of higher education. The national budget crisis, characterized as an economy in "free fall," lasted for so long that it has had long-term

impacts on how WSU, and higher education in general, will move into
the future. In July 2011, Floyd made the following statement in a letter
to the campus community:

> I am rapidly approaching my 15th year as a university President, and
> I have never encountered the succession of budget reductions that we
> are experiencing as a higher education sector and as a state.
>
> Over the past four years, WSU has realized a net state-appropriated
> budget reduction of 52 percent, or $231.0 million. These are real dollar
> reductions, and the impact has been devastating for our university. We
> have more than 500 fewer employees than when I arrived in 2007. At
> the same time, tuition has continued to rise annually by double digits.

Beyond the ongoing monitoring of programs and services that were
most critical to student success and keeping the WSU experience intact,
Floyd focused on student tuition increases. The Washington legislature
gave universities the option to levy double-digit tuition increases to make
up for the shortfall in the budget allocations. After the double-digit
increase in tuition, President Floyd assured students and parents that
WSU would hold the line on tuition increases even though its sister
institutions were set to raise tuition. After consecutive tuition increases
of 14 percent in 2009–10, 14 percent in 2010–11, 16 percent in 2011–12,
and 16 percent 2012–13, Floyd took a stance and pushed back against
the legislature. At a student rally for lower tuition, Floyd unveiled his
plan to ask the state legislature to adequately fund higher education at a
constant level while providing a slight increase. That would limit WSU
to raising tuition at the rate of the Consumer Price Index (CPI), which
was about 2 percent. In addition, Floyd gave back more than $100,000 of
his salary to the university to show his solidarity with students, faculty,
and staff at an extraordinarily challenging time.

As it turned out, Floyd successfully lobbied the legislature to provide
an overall budget increase of 12 percent, erasing the need to impose another double-digit tuition rate increase. Until his untimely death, Floyd
continued to push for WSU to improve as an institution even in light

of the budget challenges that plagued the university, and he maintained positive rapport with students, faculty, and staff.

Besides confronting the tuition crisis, President Floyd faced the decision of whether to combine the Colleges of Liberal Arts with the College of Sciences. This move would not only bring WSU in line with peer institutions, but would also serve as a cost savings mechanism given the budget challenges of the time. Relying on the work of a faculty committee of six to study the potential for this academic merger, President Floyd and Robert Bates—the provost at the time—received a detailed report on the prospect of a merger just before Thanksgiving 2007. This decision package included assessing the potential value of creating a College of Communication. The Murrow School of Communication, which fell under the College of Liberal Arts, was under consideration for full college status, which was granted in 2008.

Moving West

Elson Floyd's move to establish WSU as "Washington state's university" included increasing its presence on the west side of the state. The university's focus on assuming leadership of the Everett University Center, and building it into a campus of WSU, came as a shock to many. However, the idea of having a four-year research university in Everett and the north Puget Sound region had been in existence for more than three decades. Everett's mayor, Ray Stephanson, was a key champion for establishing a university in the local area and he was dogged in his pursuit of a four-year, public research institution to develop a home base in the region.

After seeing many opportunities to realize the dream of a university in the region slip away, Stephanson reached out to President Floyd. Floyd helped leaders in the north Puget Sound area develop an achievable plan to expand higher education. In addition to helping these leaders develop a roadmap, he brought new energy and a renewed focus on the dream.

Floyd saw the partnership with Mayor Stephanson, Everett, and other leaders in the north Puget Sound area as part of WSU's land-grant

Carmento and Elson Floyd.
Courtesy WSU Photo Services.

mission, which emphasizes providing outreach and educational opportunities to the whole state. He thought the north Puget Sound area's
challenges were an opportunity for students to improve their lives, so
they could give back to their community.

In 2011 community leaders in the north Puget Sound region came
together with Washington State University to support Senate Bill 5636
that was meant to move the fledgling Everett University Center (EUC)
under the auspices of Washington State University. The idea behind
this move was to provide the area an opportunity to move toward a
research institution within the region without the expense of starting
an entirely new university. Instead, Senate Bill 5636 would support and
allow incremental growth of the EUC into a research university and a
branch campus within the Washington State University system. Senate

Bill 5636 fully acknowledged the issue of limited access, and established parameters for transfer of the leadership, management, and operational responsibilities of the EUC from Everett Community College to Washington State University.

The legislation required WSU to develop a strategic plan for the growth and expansion of high-demand baccalaureate and graduate degree programs across the region, and for the provision of services and facilities to deliver such programs. Floyd appointed Robert J. Drewel as chancellor of WSU Everett.

WSU Everett started with programs in mechanical engineering and electrical engineering. Partnering with the robust network of community colleges in the region, students would complete the first two years of their undergraduate education with those institutions before transferring to WSU to complete their baccalaureate degree. Today WSU Everett has its first building, and the Everett University Center is growing. WSU offers degrees in hospitality business management, integrated strategic communication, software engineering, data analytics, and organic agriculture, with plans for more programs on the horizon.

In a recent interview, former mayor Ray Stephanson stated: "He understood the need for, and the value of a new facility to house new programs, new students and new opportunities for the North Puget Sound region. He was a steadfast and energetic partner who attracted many to our cause. The new building and the many students who will pass through its doors will forever be a tribute to Elson's vision and determination."

WSU's presence in Everett is about more than higher education—it will help address the region's most pressing economic challenges as we compete in a worldwide marketplace. Local businesses, large and small, rely on an economic infrastructure of industrial, commercial and professional services. Those businesses need a talented and well-trained workforce to thrive and expand.

The Tragedy in Oso, Darrington, and Arlington

Oso, Darrington and Snohomish County
have been good neighbors to WSU.
We will continue to build on
that spirit through and beyond . . .
this difficult time.

ELSON S. FLOYD

Not long after WSU began to develop its presence in Everett and the north Puget Sound region, a massive mudslide engulfed a significant portion of north Snohomish County, just east of Oso, Washington. The 2014 catastrophe took out State Route 530, destroying more than 40 structures and taking nearly 50 lives. The slide devastated the communities of Oso, Arlington, and Darrington. As the newest neighbor in the north Puget Sound, WSU moved to provide support to the community and its residents as they worked to rebuild the life that they once knew. Even as the cloud of mortality and destruction caused by the slide cast a shadow over the region and the state, the community, its leaders, and WSU came together as a ray of light that shone for this community that was struggling, but maintaining hope. There was a sincere, intense desire to bring the community back to a place of joy and hope.

Leveraging the outreach capabilities of the Snohomish County Extension office, WSU was able to assist the community in re-establishing some of its essential infrastructure and developing plans for rebuilding the community. In addition, Floyd offered to waive the tuition for all students impacted by the mudslide in the Stillaguamish Valley region. To help energize the rebuilding process, WSU Extension started an internship program for students who wanted to assist their community in rebuilding and retooling the community through work on planning, development, and general revitalization in the area. Through WSU Extension and its longstanding relationship with the three communities impacted, Floyd made a substantial, sustained, investment in helping them move past the disaster. Floyd was adamant that it was important for WSU to stand by its partners. Simply put, Floyd said, "It was the right thing to do."

MOVING ATHLETICS TO THE BIG TIME

We're in one of the most elite leagues
in the country, the Pac-10, and I am
determined we will field
competitive teams and we will have
appropriate facilities to compete in the Pac-10.

ELSON S. FLOYD

Throughout much of President Floyd's career, he saw athletics as a necessary part of the student experience on the campuses he led. But as he contemplated the future of WSU and the challenge of increasing its national and international standing, he was clear that athletics would have to play a more prominent role in the college experience and was key to building upon the strong community that made up the Cougar Nation. There were essential values that were significant to Floyd and his vision for athletics. One such value was for student-athletes to prosper academically. As a member of the Knight Commission on Intercollegiate Athletics from 2003 until 2015, Floyd spent a great deal of time discussing how to strengthen the link between sports and the educational mission of colleges and universities. In an article from the *Spokesman Review,* Floyd is quoted as saying "The landscape of college sports is changing, but no matter what happens, we want to protect the college experience and preserve the traditions that make college sports enjoyable for athletes, fans, parents and alumni. We are seizing our opportunity to usher in meaningful reform to help student-athletes and restore the academic primacy of our universities."

Floyd recognized that the opportunity to enhance WSU athletics was possible. Regent Mike Worthy said that the timing was right. "We had a visionary President that was ready to go for it, the projected revenues from the PAC-12 looked solid, the PAC-12 was gaining momentum, and the Cougar Nation wanted it to happen." Worthy's assessment of the right timing is evidenced by fact that the stature of Cougar Athletics has risen in multiple sports. "The level of competitiveness of our Athletics has been elevated significantly. Now we just need the support."

THE BILLION DOLLAR CAMPAIGN

WSU has accomplished much during this campaign.
We have constructed state-of-the-art facilities,
established and elevated top-ranking research
and academic programs, and created
new scholarships and fellowships
to improve access to higher education
for the citizens of our state.

ELSON S. FLOYD

Floyd's first billion dollar campaign was met with skepticism. Many supporters asked how could WSU possibly achieve such a lofty goal? At the start of the public phase, the campaign was close to only 30 percent of its goal, and the task seemed insurmountable. Then, with the mastery of a wizard, President Floyd brought in the most significant single donation in WSU history. Bill Gates made a gift of $25 million. That gave the campaign much needed momentum in moving toward the billion-dollar goal. Then came an unexpected windfall with the pledge of yet another record-breaking gift. Paul Allen, an alumnus of WSU, pledged a donation of $26 million, breaking the record set by Gates, his friend and former business partner. The stage was now set for WSU to move with momentum toward its final goal.

A New College of Medicine
on the Horizon

The expectation is that we will use
our medical school to improve
the quality of life for all the people
of the state of Washington.

ELSON S. FLOYD

In another show of tenacity and fortitude, Floyd pushed for WSU to establish a medical school. The single medical school in the Pacific Northwest was located at the University of Washington in Seattle, and it had the responsibility of providing medical education for five states. Floyd presented his vision to the Board of Regents and assured them that WSU had a role to play. The university would need to step forward to help provide medical education to the mass of students being denied admission to that school or who were moving out of state to receive medical training and incurring mountains of debt.

Against the odds, using finesse, strength, and persistence, Floyd was able to secure a medical school for WSU. The opposition to WSU entering the medical school space was exceptionally loud on the west side of the state. Even those who supported the effort argued that WSU's move was too soon. Floyd responded in an interview with Spokane's *Inlander* magazine: " 'There is no good reason to wait,' WSU President Elson Floyd says in a deep, precise voice. 'We've been waiting for over 100 years. It's now time to act.' " Floyd could see his best-laid plans coming to fruition. Rising to the challenge, Elson Floyd's efforts paid off once again.

Floyd spent the last five months of his life visiting the state capitol in Olympia speaking with lawmakers across the political spectrum about the significance of developing a medical school committed to providing health care to the underserved populations in eastern Washington. "He was the engine behind that bill—but it was not an easy one to get

With a map of the WSU Spokane campus on the screen behind him, Floyd makes a pitch for a new medical school to the Senate Higher Education Committee in January 2015.

Immediately after signing a bill giving WSU authority to start its own medical school in Spokane, a seated Governor Inslee is flanked by Rep. Marcus Ricelli (left), President Floyd, and Sen. Michael Baumgartner (right). *Courtesy Jim Camden.*

passed," said state Sen. Michael Baumgartner, R–Spokane. After the bill was signed, Baumgartner and others joined President Floyd in singing the WSU fight song and talked about the challenges he was facing in his battle with advanced stages of cancer. Baumgartner remarked, "I'm sure glad that he got to see that bill get passed before he went."

Closing

WSU is entering into a new era
of change and vitality. We will need
everyone's support to make this vision happen.
I want one university for and of all of
the constituents of this university . . .
with a common purpose unified around
academic excellence and preeminence.

ELSON S. FLOYD

Under Floyd's leadership, the university experienced a period of unprecedented expansion. Both President Floyd and the university have a history of being connected to and gaining strength from community. While Floyd was unable to accomplish all of his goals, his demand that WSU continue to search for innovative ways to educate students regardless of their background is central.

WSU has a long and distinguished legacy bestowed upon it by each of the great university presidents of our past. Floyd's words and actions even through times of extraordinary challenge, uncertainty, and great strife have furthered the WSU mission: "to advance knowledge through creative research, innovation, and creativity across a wide range of academic disciplines." Elson S. Floyd devoted his life to realize this mission.

Research Notes

The authors found Lee G. Bolman and Terrence E. Deal, *The Wizard and the Warrior: Leading with Passion and Power* (San Francisco: Jossey-Bass, 2016) especially relevant in analyzing Elson Floyd's leadership story. The opening quote in this chapter is drawn from B. T. Washington, *Up from Slavery: An Autobiography*. New York: Doubleday. Retrieved from www .bartleby.com/1004.

A variety of sources were accessed on the internet to help inform Floyd's biography, including websites of the Darlington School, Northwest Georgia News, the *Kalamazoo* (Michigan) *News*, Western Michigan University, University of Missouri System, the *New York Times*, and the MLive Media Group.

Washington state–based websites utilized include the *Spokesman Review*, krem.com, inlander.com, and the *Seattle Times*.

WSU-specific websites utilized include the official minutes of the WSU regents, WSU News, the *Evergreen* student newspaper, and the *Chinook* yearbooks.

Several interviews were conducted by the authors. Brian Dixon interviewed J. Fraire, May 15, 2018, and John Gardner, June 5, 2018. Paul Pitre interviewed Mike Worthy June 28, 2018.

Contributors

Scott Carson retired as the executive vice president of The Boeing Company and former president and chief executive officer of Boeing Commercial Airplanes. Carson graduated from Washington State University with a bachelor's degree in business administration. He later received a master's degree in business administration from the University of Washington. He was appointed to the WSU Board of Regents in September 2007 and also serves on the board of governors of the WSU Foundation.

Kirk H. Schulz became the 11th president of WSU and a tenured professor in the Gene and Linda Voiland School of Chemical Engineering and Bioengineering in 2016. He previously served seven years as president of Kansas State University. Prior to his appointment at KSU, President Schulz served in a variety of administrative roles during nine years at Mississippi State University. He has also served on the faculty of Michigan Technological University and the University of North Dakota. Schulz earned his undergraduate and doctoral degrees in chemical engineering at Virginia Tech.

William Stimson is a professor of journalism at Eastern Washington University. He holds a PhD in American history from Washington State University. His previous books include *Going to Washington State: A Century of Student Life* (WSU Press, 1989), *A View of the Falls: An Illustrated History of Spokane* (Windsor Publications, 1985), and *Instilling Spirit: Students and Citizenship at Washington State, 1892–1942* (WSU Press, 2015).

Mark O'English is the university archivist at Washington State University, having begun working at WSU Libraries' Manuscripts, Archives, and Special

Collections (libraries.wsu.edu/masc) in 2001. While he generally considers his own role to be preserving and providing access to university and regional history materials to help others tell those stories, he also writes regular local history columns for the regional newspapers and conducts campus history presentations for a variety of groups. Mark is a lifetime Pacific Northwesterner, by education a Beaver (bachelor's degrees in mathematics and psychology) and a Husky (master's in library science), and now by vocation a Cougar. In addition to northwest history, he's written extensively for reference works for Marvel Publishing and other publishers.

Tim Steury, like Enoch Bryan, is a Hoosier farm boy who came west for academic opportunities and became enamored of its land and culture. He joined WSU in 1990 as research news coordinator and editor of the research magazine *Universe*. He created *Ask Dr. Universe*, an online and newspaper science question-and-answer column for kids of all ages, and is a founding editor of *Washington State Magazine*. He retired from WSU in 2014 and with his wife Diane Noel currently raises hogs, pears, and heritage dessert and cider apples near Potlatch, Idaho.

Trevor James Bond is the codirector of the Center for Digital Scholarship and Curation and the associate dean for Digital Initiatives and Special Collections at the Washington State University Libraries. He received his master's in library and information science with a specialization in archives and preservation management and a master's in ancient history at UCLA. He completed his doctorate at WSU in the Department of History in 2017.

Larry Clark has served as editor of *Washington State Magazine*, the quarterly publication of Washington State University, since 2014. He previously worked as a writer, editor, and communications professional at magazines, nonprofits, state government, and corporations for over 15 years. He graduated from WSU in 1994 with a bachelor's degree in journalism from the Edward R. Murrow School of Communication, and a second bachelor's degree in Asian studies. He earned a master's degree from the University of Oregon in Asian studies.

Sam Fleischer is a doctoral student in modern American history at Washington State University. He has been teaching collegiate education, English, and history courses for over twenty years across the United States, and is also a prolific freelance journalist. On the side, he is an Ironman triathlete and a certified triathlon coach.

John T. Menard is currently a graduate student in the history department at WSU. He also holds a bachelor's degree in history from WSU. He previously worked as a high school world history and economics teacher, as well as a book reviewer for the *Yakima Herald-Republic*. His other professional writing includes an article on the North Idaho Civilian Conservation Corps in *Columbia* magazine and a forthcoming manuscript on the birth of the craft beer industry in eastern Washington.

Brian Stack is currently a doctoral candidate in history at Washington State University where he also earned his master's degree in history in 2015 under the supervision of Dr. Peter Boag. Despite growing up in New England and doing undergraduate work at the University of Rhode Island, Brian is now firmly planted on the West Coast. His dissertation examines the interrelated histories of the American West, sexuality, and animal abuse during the twentieth century. His other works have focused on local and university histories, especially focused on lesbian and gay student activism and organizations.

Buddy Levy is a clinical professor of English at Washington State University. He is the author of *Labyrinth of Ice: The Triumphant and Tragic Greely Polar Expedition* (St. Martin's Press, 2019), *No Barriers: A Blind Man's Journey to Kayak the Grand Canyon* (with Erik Weihenmayer; Thomas Dunne Books, 2017), *Geronimo: The Life and Times of An American Warrior* (co-authored with Coach Mike Leach, Simon & Schuster, 2014), *River of Darkness: Francisco Orellana's Legendary Voyage of Death and Discovery Down the Amazon* (Bantam Dell, 2011), *Conquistador: Hernan Cortes, King Montezuma, and the Last Stand of the Aztecs* (Bantam Dell, 2008), *American Legend: The Real-Life Adventures of David Crockett* (Putnam, 2005, Berkley Books, 2006), and *Echoes*

On Rimrock: In Pursuit of the Chukar Partridge (Pruett, 1998). Levy is also a freelance writer, speaker, and dabbler in the entertainment industry.

Paul Pitre became chancellor for Washington State University's Everett campus in September 2016, after serving as academic dean of the campus from 2011 to 2016. He is an associate professor of educational leadership and counseling psychology at WSU. He was previously a member of the Auburn University faculty. Pitre has worked in public affairs for the Greater Seattle Chamber of Commerce and as a program management analyst at the U.S. Department of Education. He received his doctorate in education policy and leadership from the University of Maryland, a master's degree in higher education administration from New York University, and his bachelor's degree in communication studies from Western Washington University.

Aaron Ngozi Oforlea is an associate professor of English at Washington State University. He has published several articles in the areas of African American literature, folklore, and masculinity and a book entitled *James Baldwin, Toni Morrison: The Rhetorics of Black Male Subjectivity*. Currently, he is exploring the intersections of narrative, medicine, critical race theory, and African American literature.

Brian Dixon is assistant vice president of Student Financial Services at WSU. Originally from Wisconsin, Brian received his bachelor's degree in political science at the University of Wisconsin–Madison before beginning his higher education career at his alma mater in the admissions department. Additionally, he earned a master's degree in business administration from Cardinal Stritch University and is completing a doctorate in higher education leadership and policy at Concordia University in Portland, Oregon. Before his time at WSU, Brian served as the vice president of business development at Collegiate Consulting in Louisiana. He has also worked as a systems manager in financial aid and scholarships at the University of Wisconsin–Parkside and as a financial aid advisor at the University of Wisconsin–Milwaukee.

Index

Page numbers in italic indicate photographs.